UNBEARABLE
BURDEN

UNBEARABLE BURDEN

*One Mother's Decision
to Trust God When He Asked
the Impossible*

KRISTA M. ISAACSON

Edited by Tristi Pinkston
Published by Red Rims Press
kristamisaacson@gmail.com

Cover Design: Shaustia Brown and Francine Platt
Cover Photo: Belinda Olsen
Interior book design: Francine Platt • EdenGraphics.net

All interior photos taken and used with permission
by the Isaacson family

Paperback edition: 979-8-9855775-0-1

eBook: 979-8-9855775-1-8

Printed in the United States of America

"*Unbearable Burden* is a beautifully written story that captures the tender and sacred experiences that only come during the harrowing reality of watching the death of a child. Krista's heartbreak and sorrow are present in every passage, yet her faith and courage to put her will in God's hands every step of the way of losing her sweet Elora is a consecrated testimony of how such a burden becomes holy."

— MICHELLE SCHMIDT AND ANGIE TAYLOR, coauthors of *Carried: How One Mother's Trust in God Helped Her through the Unthinkable.*

"Though the author and her family carried the unbearable burden of letting go of their sweet Elora, readers will be blessed for investing time in this beautiful story. From experiencing heartache, tender mercies from God, and seeing glimpses of heaven, I am a better person for having read this book. No parent would want to be in the position Krista and her husband faced, but all parents should read their experiences as a reminder to live and love in every moment."

— JODI ORGILL BROWN, award-winning author of *The Sun Still Shines*

"*Unbearable Burden* is a touching, well-written story about trial, loss, and heartache. While we may not know why tragedies happen, this book shows the Lord is there to guide us forward and help shoulder our burdens along the way. A poignant reminder that even in our darkest moments, God keeps His promises and will help us find peace."

- ABEL KEOGH, author of *Room for Two*

DEDICATION

To all the hands who held me together
when my world fell apart.
Especially my Travis,
who daily keeps his original promise.

– KMI

CONTENTS

*...may God grant unto you
that your burdens may be light,
through the joy of his Son.*

ALMA 33:23

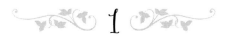

1

A GLANCE

THE SOCIAL WORKER said we should take the stairs. It was the only way my husband and I might have one last chance to see our daughter.

"This way. Hurry."

Jennifer had been a hospital social worker long enough to know the shortcuts. She rushed us down an obscure hallway, through a heavy door with a push-bar handle, and into a barren white stairwell. I raced behind her, jumping stairs two at a time, with my husband, Travis, hard on my heels. Up two floors. Through another heavy door. Into a long corridor lined with hospital equipment.

Please let us be in time.

"The operating room is through those double doors ahead. If we stand right here, you'll be able to see Elora as they run past."

I pressed my back against the wall, making sure I wouldn't be in the way. My whole body shook with a shivering, painful tremor that ached in my jaw and stabbed at my gut. Travis noticed and grabbed my hand. It helped. But I still needed to find a way to stay in control for a few more minutes. Reaching deep into the well of my soul, I scratched and clawed for any fragment of strength that remained.

God? I need you. Please, please hold me together.

"Be ready." Jennifer tried to prepare us. "It will be fast. You'll probably only get a glance."

It didn't matter. If it was the last time I ever saw Elora alive, a glance would be priceless.

Ding.

Elevator doors opened.

Voices shouted orders.

A mass of bodies in green scrubs wheeled the gurney out of the elevator, made a hard left, and started running.

One nurse held an IV bag high in the air.

Another knelt on the bed, doing chest compressions on Elora's tiny unclothed body.

I choked down the terror and forced myself not to look away. With all my soul, I needed to see Elora's face. I frantically scanned the spaces between the blur of arms and heads flying past.

There. A flash of auburn hair. An eye, mostly closed. A manual air pump pressed over her nose and mouth.

A microscopic glance, and then...

She was gone.

Through doors where I could not follow.

Please, God, go with her. And let her know I'm right here.

That prayer was the only thing left in the world I could do for her.

Except cry.

2

SLOPES

LOOKING BACK, I can pinpoint the exact day God set me on the path that would lead to standing helplessly outside Elora's operating room. It was almost one year earlier on a cold but sunny January morning. The day I learned to ski.

Travis gripped the minivan's steering wheel with both hands and bounced in his seat, wearing his biggest toothy grin.

"You're ridiculous," I teased.

"I can't help it! I've wanted to take you skiing for so long!"

It was true. And I'd been making excuses out of fear for just as long. "I only hope I don't fall getting off the chairlift."

"Well, if you do, I promise I'll help you up."

I knew he would, but my stomach churned anyway. Skiing sounded cold, wet, and unpredictable. But I loved my husband, and he loved to ski. I wanted to try.

We parked the car, bought our lift passes, and carried our gear to the top of the bunny hill. Travis helped me strap down my boots and lock them into my skis. He skied backward in front of me while I inched my way down the resort's easiest slope. I only fell once.

"Okay," I said when I reached the bottom, "I can see why you like this."

Travis smiled that goofy grin again.

Krista's First Time on Skis
January 2006

After a few more times down the bunny hill, practicing wedge-shaped "pizza" formations with my skis to come to a stop and parallel ski "French fries" to go faster, Travis said I was ready to try a *real* run. I skied down an easy green-level course four times without falling, then asked, "What's next?" with an eagerness that surprised both me and my husband.

4

Travis wasn't sure if there were any other beginner slopes, so he asked a guide standing near a map of the resort for a recommendation.

"There's a pretty easy blue run. It starts off kinda steep, but finishes out like a green."

Travis looked at me like he wasn't too sure. "Think you're ready for that? We can just stick to the green run today."

"Nah, that's boring. Let's do it!"

We rode a fast-moving chairlift to the top of the mountain and followed signs to the head of the blue run—a steep ledge that overlooked a giant snowy bowl lined on both sides with thick groves of towering pines.

I watched skiers plunge down the steep slope, cross the base of the bowl, and glide back up the opposite side. Up and down, side to side, like marbles rolling in a dish until a narrow neck at the bottom of the bowl funneled them out to gentler terrain.

Travis threw a protective arm in front of me.

"Before you go, I want to teach you a couple of things."

I nodded. "Good idea."

"Don't go barreling straight down. Go back and forth across the slope." He traced a safe path in the air with his hand. "And if you get going too fast and you feel out of control, just sit down. It's better than having a bad fall."

"Sit down. I can do that."

"Are you ready?"

"Absolutely." So, I went.

And I did exactly what he said not to.

I couldn't steer. Couldn't turn to the side. Couldn't stop.

"Pizza! Pizza!" Travis yelled from behind. But pizzas weren't working. I was going too fast.

I might have made it safely to the gentler slope ahead if not for the elderly gentleman who unknowingly skied into my path. It was clear that I wouldn't be able to stop without plowing him over, so I followed Travis's advice. I sat down.

And it worked—until momentum carried me toward a soft snow pile at the side of the run. My right ski stuck firmly in the snow while the rest of my body continued to slide.

I heard the pop first, then hot pain tore through my knee.

Travis was immediately at my side.

I sucked air through gritted teeth. "Babe, it hurts."

"What can I do?" Travis asked, his voice thick with worry.

I breathed rapidly, trying to get a handle on the pain. The weight of the ski and boot pulled painfully on my knee.

"My skis. I can't get 'em off."

As quickly as he could, Travis pressed the release levers at the base of my heels, and both skis fell away. I held my right knee to my chest, rocking back and forth until the pain subsided.

"Ahh, I think it's okay now. Man, that hurt."

"Think you can get up? We need to move so we don't get run over."

"Yeah. I think so."

Travis supported me while I stood and gently tested my knee. "How does it feel?"

"A bit tender, but not too bad."

"Do you want to try to ski out?"

"Well, I'm not *walking* down this mountain. Let's go."

Travis laughed and put my skis on the ground in front of me.

I placed the tip of my right boot into the binding, but as I pressed my heel down to lock the boot in place, my knee turned to Jell-O. It wobbled and bowed to the side like my bones had disappeared.

"Ooo. That's not right." My stomach lurched.

"What? What happened?"

"My knee. It's all wobbly. I think I might throw up." I could feel the blood draining from my face.

I leaned forward and breathed. Travis pressed himself against my side and rubbed my back. When the nausea passed, I stood tall and jammed my heel down as hard as I could. And then again, even harder.

"I can't push hard enough to lock in my boot."

Travis spun his head around, searching the area. "Can you walk?"

"I don't know."

He pointed to a pine tree in the middle of the run that would lend us some protection from the other skiers flying down the hill. "Can you make it that far?"

"I'll try."

One step forward, and my knee buckled under my weight. Travis took off his skis and wrapped my left arm around his shoulder. Together we hobbled to the tree. I sat down heavily under the canopy of branches with my back to the trunk. Travis hurried back up the hill to retrieve our skis and poles.

"Trav, I don't know how I'm gonna get down."

"Yeah, I know. What if I left you here and skied down to get help?"

"I think you might have to."

"I really don't like leaving you here alone, though."

"I'll be fine. You won't be that long."

"I still don't like it." He stood by the tree, looking up and down the slope, deliberating.

Just then, a man on a snowmobile came over the ridge and

stopped beside us. He wore a bright red coat with white crosses on the sleeves. "Everything all right?"

"My wife hurt her knee," Travis answered.

"How bad is it?"

"She can't walk or get her ski back on."

"I just got a call to go pick up another injury farther down, and it's more serious. Can you wait? How are you feeling?" He bent his head low until he could see my face under the branches.

I smiled. "I'm fine. Just feel stupid."

"Okay, I'll radio the patrol station. It shouldn't be too long." He detached a walkie-talkie from the shoulder strap of his coat, relayed the information about my injury and location, then sped off in search of the other injured skier.

Travis stood watch, ready to flag down the help when it arrived.

Ten minutes passed. My legs were numb from sitting so long in the snow, but they didn't bother me as much as my pride.

What was I thinking? Skiing a blue run on my first day. I should have listened to Travis and stayed on the easier slopes. Then I wouldn't be sitting here in the snow, waiting for someone to haul me off this mountain. I started to cry.

Travis knelt beside me. "Does your knee hurt?"

"No. I just feel really bad."

"About what?"

"I ruined our day."

"What are you talking about? You didn't ruin anything."

"Yes, I did. I shouldn't have pushed you to take me down this run. And now I'm hurt and we can't ski anymore, and..." I slumped my shoulders, not knowing what else to say, tears turning icy on my frozen cheeks.

Travis put his arm around me and squeezed. "Listen to me. Are you listening?"

I nodded.

"Today has been one of the most fun days of my life. And even if we're just sitting here in the snow, I'd rather be with you than anywhere else in the world."

I kissed him.

Moments later, a member of the ski patrol swooshed to a stop next to my tree. He was harnessed to a long red toboggan.

You've got to be kidding me.

"Oh, I thought they were sending another snowmobile." Travis read my mind.

"They're being used on other parts of the mountain," Ski Patrol explained.

That toboggan was my only way out. So I took a deep breath, left my pride in the snow, and climbed aboard.

One long, but impressively fast toboggan ride later, Ski Patrol delivered me safely to the small outbuilding that served as the resort's medical clinic. The doctor tested my knee, bending it and then straightening it at different angles, taking note when I breathed sharply or grimaced.

"You've definitely torn something. My guess is your meniscus, the lining under your kneecap. But it could also be your ACL, and a ligament tear is more serious. But without X-rays or an MRI, it's impossible to know what's really wrong."

The doctor strapped my knee into a bright blue leg brace, wrote a prescription for pain meds, and sent me home with a referral to an orthopedic surgeon.

Travis supported me across the icy parking lot to the car, no longer wearing his toothy grin from that morning. The drive home was laced with worries. *X-rays? MRI? Surgery?* How was I going to take care of my family?

Four little voices yelled my name as I limped through the front door. They raced to be the first to hug me, but the three oldest stopped short when they noticed the brace around my leg. Two-year-old Elora either didn't notice or didn't care and threw her arms around my knees. Already unsteady on my feet, her tiny love attack knocked me sideways. I reached out a hand to steady myself against the doorframe, wincing as a zing of pain shot from knee to hip.

Travis's mom appeared around the corner from the kitchen. "Oh, no! What happened?"

"Krista was a daredevil skier," Travis joked.

"I'm fine." I smiled so the kids wouldn't worry. "Just a little accident."

Sweet seven-year-old Shaustia ran into my arms. Five-year-old Walker came too. Shaustia asked, "Are you okay?"

"I will be."

Caleb, the logical oldest child, wasn't satisfied. "What *really* happened?"

Travis told the thrilling tale while he helped me to the couch and propped a cushion under my leg. Elora crawled up and sat on my stomach. I squished her tight.

"Mommy? Ca' I has milk?"

"Yes, but Mommy can't get up, so Daddy will help you."

She slid to the floor, grabbed Travis's finger, and pulled him into the kitchen.

Stupid. Reckless. I draped my arm over my eyes so they wouldn't see me crying.

Two days later, I hobbled into the orthopedic surgeon's office, still wearing the leg brace. After examining my knee, the doctor confirmed I had torn something, and scheduled me for surgery.

An admissions representative from the hospital called the following morning to get me pre-registered, asking questions about insurance and my personal medical history.

"Are you currently taking any medication?"

"No."

"Do you smoke?"

"No."

"Are you, or could you be, pregnant?"

"N..." The word nearly flew from my mouth, but a voice in my head whispered, *Maybe you should check.*

"Umm...Can I call you back tomorrow?"

"Yes." I could feel her smile through the phone. "That will be fine."

Travis brought home a pregnancy test, and the next morning I called the admissions office to report the results.

"So, it turns out I *am* pregnant." I was still in shock. I hadn't said those words out loud yet to anyone but Travis.

Baby number five.

Travis and I were excited about adding another child to our family, but I was also a bit apprehensive about the timing. Pregnancy and injury aren't the best companions.

The woman on the other end of the call, however, was nothing but overjoyed. "Oh, that's such great news! Congratulations!"

"Thanks! Crazy way to find out, though, huh?"

"For sure. So... I guess that means we'll see you in a year."

"I'm sorry. What?"

"Sweetheart, if you're pregnant, no surgeon will touch you with a ten-foot pole."

My brain went fuzzy. "But…I have four kids. And I can't walk."

"I know, Mrs. Isaacson. But the most important thing is to keep you and baby safe. And that means waiting."

I couldn't think how to respond.

"Will you be all right?" she asked.

"I guess I'll figure something out."

"Take care, honey." And she hung up.

I set my phone on the coffee table.

A year?

Travis came home from work to find me surrounded by damp hills of used tissues.

"I don't get it!" I cried. "Why pregnant and hurt at the same time? Couldn't God have let me get pregnant last month? Then I wouldn't have gone skiing at all. Or… couldn't He have stopped me from getting pregnant until after my surgery? I don't understand the timing. I mean, one week…my surgery would be over, and everything would be fine."

"I don't know, babe," Travis said, trying his best to calm me, "but that sounds like the perfect question to pray about."

"I have been. But I'm so scared about everything, I can't hear if God's answering. Think you could give me a blessing?"

A priesthood blessing—a prayer of healing and counsel from God.

"Of course I will." Travis stood next to me and placed his hands on my head.

Through Travis, God promised that my knee would soon heal enough for me to take care of my family. But He explained that if I hadn't been hurt, I never would have asked for this blessing, and there was something I needed to hear. The baby joining our family had been sent at this exact time for a very specific reason. God's timing had a purpose. I needed to trust Him.

Travis finished the blessing, and I stopped crying.

God hadn't shown me the future—hadn't warned me away from the black abyss He could see ahead. My life rested safely at the top of a slope, oblivious to the avalanche about to barrel me over the edge. Only God knew how excruciating the fall would be. But all He asked was that I trust Him.

...Be not afraid, only believe.

MARK 5:36

3

MISCHIEF

B Y EARLY SPRING, I had put the blue leg brace away in a closet. My knee wasn't perfect, but it really only bothered me going up and down stairs. Pregnancy morning sickness had mostly subsided as well, and I was finally able to care for my family at full capacity—just as God had promised. Travis had done a wonderful job filling in for me while I recovered, but he was exhausted. Working his full-time job while managing a houseful of four busy little mess-makers had been a lot to handle.

Especially with Elora in the mix.

Elora was a stealthy, curious two-year-old, a dangerous combination. She'd been drawn to mischief from the moment she learned to crawl.

My sister-in-law and I had an ongoing competition. We called each other nearly every day to see whose toddler had gotten into more trouble. Elora didn't always win, but she did on the day I found her clinging to the very top shelf of the pantry where the fruit snacks were stored. Also, on the day she ate all of the pink fluoride tablets out of the bottle and I had to call the Poison Control Center. And again, on the day she picked every single leaf off my favorite houseplant, leaving it a barren stick that never recovered.

She was a talented troublemaker, but there was one "victory" that forever put her other mischief to shame.

Summer was well underway. Caleb and Walker were overdue for haircuts, so I got out the clippers and set a stool in the middle of the kitchen floor.

Fifteen minutes later, Caleb's thick brown mop was freshly buzzed and he headed to the bathroom. His newest nine-year-old habit was to take overly long showers. "Make it fast!" I called. "Walker's coming in right behind you!"

As I made the first pass with the clippers through Walker's copper-red mane, Elora wandered into the kitchen, fascinated by the clumps of hair scattered on the floor. Knowing the mess it would make if she traipsed through them, I scooted her out of the room and asked Shaustia to keep an eye on her.

As soon as I was finished, I set the clippers on the floor and carried Walker to the shower so he wouldn't track loose hair all over the carpet. In the few minutes I was gone, Elora escaped Shaustia's watchful eye and snuck into the kitchen. I was on my way back from the bathroom to sweep up the kitchen floor when Elora came running through the doorway smack into my legs.

"What have you been up to, little one?" I asked.

She didn't answer, but kept her head tipped down, a slight frown in the corners of her mouth, peering up at me through long eyelashes—her signature look that meant she'd done something she shouldn't. I knelt down and inspected her hands and feet. Nothing. They were clean. But as I looked back up at her face, it was her hair that caught my eye. I'd worked hard that morning to comb, smooth, and gel it into two perfect ponytails. Now it looked like Elora had snagged her hair on something and pulled.

"What did you do to your ponytails?"

No reply.

"Well, let Mommy fix them and then you can go play, okay?" She nodded.

I grasped the soft elastic band around one ponytail and pulled. Out it came—along with a thick section of Elora's beautiful auburn hair.

"What in the world...?" That's when I remembered the clippers.

I pulled the elastic from the second ponytail. More hair. She had managed to turn on the clippers and buzz the hair all along the front of her head.

The irreparable clippings lay draped over my hand, Elora's long, gorgeous hair reduced to a horrendous mullet. I didn't know what to do.

Cry? Laugh? Yell?

I was a mixed bag of emotions until I realized that Elora hadn't taken her eyes off me.

She was quietly watching to see how I would react, fear clouding the sparkle in her big blue eyes. A clear thought entered my mind.

She loves you. She trusts you. Don't ruin that.

I brushed my fingers over her fuzzy stubs of buzzed hair. With a sigh of resignation, I tipped her chin up and smiled to reassure her I wasn't angry. Her face lit up into a wide-mouthed grin. Such a beautiful smile beneath such a ridiculous haircut, I couldn't help myself. I started to laugh. I laughed and hugged

Elora and laughed harder until I could barely breathe.

And then I did what any sensible woman would do—I called my mother.

When she answered the phone, I was laughing too hard to talk.

Mom started to panic. "Are you laughing or crying?"

"Both!" I burst out, then laughed hard for several more seconds before I could calm down enough to tell her about Elora's shaved head. "Mom, it's *so* bad! What should I do?"

"It's simple," she replied. "Make sure you take lots of pictures."

I hung up the phone, put Elora's ponytails back in, led her by the hand into the kitchen, handed her the hair clippers, and took the most adorable pictures of my mischievous girl.

Laughter. It was the right decision.

The time for tears would come soon enough.

Mischief Elora, 2 years old
July 25, 2006

4

AN EXCITING MORNING

SIX MONTHS after her head-shaving incident, Elora's hair still hadn't fully grown back. Her short, uneven bangs were impossible to tame and even harder to hide. Most days I didn't mind what other people thought, but as the middle of January approached, I wished her hair had grown out a little faster. My husband's youngest brother, McKay, had been away for two years in Mexico serving a proselytizing mission for our church. Elora was a baby when he left. I'd hoped to reintroduce Elora to him minus the mullet.

Homecoming day dawned cold, but sunny. I jumped out of bed without pushing snooze on the alarm clock and kissed Travis on the cheek. Four-month-old baby Noah slept quietly in his bassinet next to my bed, so I tiptoed from the room and started rousing the other children. Caleb, Shaustia, and Walker were so excited that they dressed themselves and made their beds without complaint while I helped Elora. She was very particular about the clothes she wanted to wear to the airport—pink T-shirt, jeans, and her favorite Winnie the Pooh shoes. I thought about forcing her into one of the flowery headbands we'd bought to hide her wild bangs, but she hated them, and I decided it wasn't worth the fight.

Our family on the day we brought baby Noah home from the hospital
Travis, Elora, Caleb, Shaustia, Walker, Noah, Krista
September 2006

I carried her with me into the kitchen to fix breakfast. Once everyone had eaten their fill of buttermilk pancakes, I grabbed our stack of homemade "Welcome Home" signs and helped the family pile into the minivan.

We drove into the airport parking garage with plenty of time to spare. The three oldest children spotted their grandparents and cousins walking across the parking lot and ran ahead to meet them. Travis carried Noah, and he and I each held one of Elora's hands.

"Swing me!" she said.

Travis and I grinned at each other. "One, two, three, wheee!" we chanted in unison, then swung her by the arms into the air.

She squealed in delight. "Again!"

We swung Elora all the way across the parking lot, enjoying her contagious laughter. One more swing over the crosswalk, up onto the sidewalk, and suddenly Elora's laugh was gone. As she landed, she started whining, trying to pull her hand out of mine.

"Elora, you can't let go of Mommy! There are too many cars!"

I tightened my grasp and kept walking. She cried and yanked harder on my hand. I couldn't understand this sudden change in emotions, so I knelt down beside her.

"Elora, what's the matter, baby?"

"My shoe!" she cried in despair, pointing back toward the parking lot.

There in the middle of the crosswalk lay a favorite Winnie the Pooh shoe. I ran back, retrieved it, put it on her foot, and wiped the tears from her face. She was content, but wanted nothing more to do with swinging.

A large group of extended family members had congregated in the airport's main concourse. Someone announced that McKay's plane had landed, so we formed a wide semi-circle and held up our signs, scanning every face that came through the terminal exit.

Elora was very proud to have her own sign. It read, "Remember Me?" She stood proudly, crazy-haired, smiling over the edge of the cardboard, even though I suspected she had no idea what all the fuss was about.

When McKay appeared, everyone cheered and took turns hugging him. Elora kept that huge smile on her face until the moment McKay knelt down in front of her. As he reached out to shake her hand, she dropped her sign and hid behind my leg. It took some gentle coaxing before she braved a peek to say hello. He never even noticed her hair.

Elora meeting her Uncle McKay
January 18, 2007

While McKay made his way through the group hugging and chatting and snapping pictures, I picked up Elora and found a chair away from the crowd where I could snuggle her. It wasn't long before the other kids complained they were bored listening to all of the grown-ups talk, and asked if they could ride the escalator with their cousins.

"Yes," I told them. "But no goofing off. And stay out of people's way. Promise?"

They all bobbed their heads profusely and hurried away.

Elora watched them board the escalator. "I go too?" she asked.

"No, sweetie. You're too little."

She pouted. A few seconds later, she asked again with perfect puppy-dog eyes, "I go, peez?"

I couldn't resist her. "Okay. Go play. But stay by Shaustia."

She ran to the base of the escalator, timidly put her foot out in front of her, then hopped aboard the moving steps. She grinned, rode all the way to the top, did a little happy dance, walked around the handrail, and rode the escalator back down.

As soon as she was safely back at the bottom, she looked in my direction and called out, "Mommy! You see me?"

And I did.

The way she ran and played and laughed and smiled. Her funny hair, her Winnie the Pooh shoes, and her big blue eyes.

I saw her. And never suspected she was anything other than happy and well.

Teach me to do thy will;
for thou art my God: thy spirit is good;
lead me into the land of uprightness.

PSALM 143:10

5

A WORRISOME AFTERNOON

TRAVIS'S MOM suggested we move the airport homecoming party to her house. Travis needed to go to work and caught a ride with his uncle after helping me load the kids back into the van.

The kids and I spent an enjoyable afternoon with the family. McKay thrilled us with stories from his mission about crazy regional cuisine, rabid dogs, and the wonderful Mexican people he'd met. We stuffed ourselves with barbecue meatballs, seven-layer dip, mini deli sandwiches, cream puffs, chocolate chip cookies, and bowls filled with candy. The kids played outside on the swing set and made snowballs from slushy piles in the corners of the yard, enjoying every minute of cousin time.

Elora was her usual self, caught hiding in a corner of the kitchen under a chair with two cookies in each hand, and later, under the table, cheeks bulging with M&Ms, and even later, in a corner of the sunroom scarfing a huge chunk of brownie. Her chocolate-smeared grin was so adorable, no one scolded her, but I knew the evening would most likely end with a two-year-old bellyache.

Toward late afternoon, I announced to my children that it was time to head home. Even though I hated to take them away from their cousins, I had a church meeting I'd promised to attend. We hugged and kissed the family goodbye with promises of seeing everyone soon. Minutes later, all five kids had fallen asleep in the car. I drove in contented silence toward a brilliant orange sun setting over a golden Utah Lake.

Caleb, Shaustia, and Walker all woke as the van tires bounced over the curb of our driveway. Caleb carried baby Noah into the house while I unhooked Elora from her car seat and cradled her on my shoulder. I laid her on my bed where she could keep sleeping, then changed out of my jeans into a knee-length brown skirt. Closing the bedroom door behind me, I went into the kitchen to fix a quick dinner.

I was serving grilled cheese and baby carrots to the older kids when Elora came wobbling into the kitchen, groggy from her late nap. She rubbed at her eyes angrily as they adjusted to the brightness of the room. Catching sight of me, she extended her arms, asking to be held.

"Come over here, Elora. Mommy's cooking." But she couldn't. Each time she tried to steer her body in my direction, she tipped to the side, almost falling over. Her legs refused to walk in a straight line. She cried louder and louder with frustration.

Poor thing. She must really be tired.

I stepped away from the counter and picked her up. "Ohhh-kay. Shhh. You thirsty?"

She nodded, but didn't stop crying.

I sat her on the edge of the counter and filled a sippy cup with milk. She reached out to take it, but a tremor in her hands made it difficult to get a good grip.

That's weird.

Maybe she was just shivery, cold after being wrapped in the covers on my bed. I asked Shaustia to bring me a blanket, wrapped Elora up, put her on my left hip, and scooped a sandwich off the griddle.

Elora whimpered, "No, Mommy," as I tried to coax a bite of food into her mouth.

"All right, sweetheart. Mommy will just hold you."

Thirty minutes later, Elora still hadn't settled down.

We were back in the van on our way to the babysitter's house. My friend Tara had agreed to watch the four older kids while I was at my meeting. Elora cried, a thin lethargic whine that stretched over the length of each breath. Her head rested wearily against the side of her car seat. Shaustia tried singing songs and playing "I Spy" out the window, but Elora paid no attention. I thought back to the treats she'd eaten at the party. Maybe the predicted bellyache had reared its head after all. By the time we arrived at Tara's, I was no longer sure that leaving Elora was such a good idea.

Caleb, Shaustia, and Walker rushed right into the house to play, but as I carried Elora to the front door, she threw her arms around my neck and sobbed, "No, Mommy! No, Mommy!" The sudden desperation in her voice tore at my heart.

Tara volunteered to hold Elora for a minute to see if she would calm down. I passed her into Tara's arms, but that only made things worse. Elora panicked—arms stretched out to me, coughing and gagging as she screamed, wrenching backward, begging with her whole body for me to hold her again.

"Krista, you can go. I'm sure she'll be fine after a few minutes."

But I couldn't. Something inside warned me I would regret

it if I did. Nearly crying myself, I reached out my arms and told Tara, "I'll just take her with me. She's *way* more important than this meeting." Elora dove back into my arms. She buried her face in my neck and began to settle.

After thanking Tara for watching the other kids, I carried Elora back to the car, her breath ragged and shaky, the remnants of a hard cry.

Back in the driver's seat, I glanced at the clock.

Already five minutes late. Maybe I should just cancel.

It was probably the right decision, but I couldn't move past my perceived obligation.

Maybe a compromise? Stay for a few minutes, find out about any new assignments, then make my excuses and take Elora home.

It sounded like the perfect plan.

I parked the van as close to the church doors as possible, slung the diaper bag over my shoulder, bundled Noah in a blanket on one hip, and wrapped Elora in her coat on the other. I walked carefully over the frozen pavement, then with one finger and a foot, managed to open the double glass doors and maneuver myself through.

Voices sounded inside a room right off the lobby. Luckily, the door hadn't been closed all the way. I nudged it open with my shoulder and bumbled inside.

All seven women in the room laughed and jumped up to lend me a hand. One grabbed me a chair, and another volunteered to hold Noah. I dropped into my seat with Elora on my lap and let the diaper bag fall off my shoulder to the floor.

"I'm sorry I'm so late. I didn't expect..." But before I got the words out, Elora, laying on my shoulder, made a terrible gagging noise and threw up all down the front of both of us.

I jumped to my feet and pressed her tightly against me to contain the mess. The nearest bathroom was clear down a carpeted hallway, so I bolted outside. The winter air was bitter without my coat, but even worse for Elora. As I stood her on the ground to assess the mess, her tiny body shivered violently, and I berated myself for not listening to my earlier instincts.

"Oh, sweetness, Mommy's so sorry!" I needed to get her home.

The door behind me opened and my friend Liz appeared, carrying baby Noah, the diaper bag, and the coats.

"Liz, I shouldn't have come! I thought Elora might be feeling sick, but I didn't want to miss the meeting, and now—"

"Stop." Liz cut me off. "Every woman here is a mom too. We've all been there. Right now, the only important thing is that you go home and take care of your family. Come on—I'll help you to your car."

I wrapped myself tightly around Elora despite the mess.

Liz dug the van keys from my coat pocket, unlocked the doors, started the engine and heater, and buckled Noah into his seat. I stood Elora inside the open sliding door where the heater could warm her while I tried to clean her up.

"Need anything else?" Liz asked.

I yanked a baby wipe from its plastic container and cleaned Elora's hands. "Just call me tomorrow and tell me what I missed, okay?"

Liz promised, then headed back inside the church.

Despite the warmth of the heater, Elora's body wouldn't stop shaking. She cried as I wiped her face, arms, and shirt, not soothed by my whispers that everything was going to be all right.

When the baby wipes had done all they could, I tried to

buckle Elora into her car seat. She fought and screamed, wanting only to stay in my arms. I didn't know what to do. I was all alone, in the freezing dark, with a child who needed to get home but refused to cooperate. And I was starting to feel panicked.

Heavenly Father, I need help. I've got to get Elora home.

For a brief moment, Elora quieted. Seizing the opportunity, I quickly buckled her, then jumped into the driver's seat. She wailed, but at least she was safe. I drove anxiously through the darkness, cooing to her in the tipped-down rearview mirror, "It's okay, baby girl. We're almost home."

She would not be consoled.

6

A DEVASTATING NIGHT

A SURPRISED TARA met me at the door, but one look at my shirt told her why I was back so soon to pick up my kids. She gathered their shoes and jackets, helped them into the van, and waved her well-wishes from the front porch as we drove away.

Finally home, Elora and I showered and dressed in clean clothes. Caleb, Shaustia, and Walker helped each other get ready for bed. I let them watch a movie downstairs while they waited for the out-of-town cousins who were planning to spend the night at our house.

Elora fell asleep in my arms. I held her for a while, humming lullabies, but when Noah woke up, ready to be fed, I tucked Elora between the pink sheets of her bed.

I sat on the couch to nurse Noah, but soon heard Elora cry out, "Mommy!" followed by a gagging cough. I hurried into the room and laid Noah in his crib, ignoring his crying protests to his interrupted meal. Elora sat upright in bed, covered in vomit, shivering harder than before. I bathed her, changed her, and snuggled her beside me wrapped in a blanket while I finished feeding the baby.

Elora threw up four more times over the next two hours, coughing mess into her hair and soiling her clothes. When there were no more clean pajamas, I put her in one of my own shirts, a green-striped tee with a small pocket sewn to the left chest. It nearly reached her ankles. The fabric carried my scent, and I hoped it would help soothe her.

Elora was now too weak to walk on her own, and my worry gnawed at my stomach. She cried thinly, head on my shoulder, arms limp at her sides as I carried her to my bed. Propped up on one elbow, I lay down beside her, keeping vigil, my hand on her chest measuring its rise and fall. Finally, she fell into a deep, exhausted sleep.

The front door opened, and Travis's brother Jared and his family tiptoed into the house. I called quietly from my bedroom that Elora wasn't feeling well, so they just waved goodnight and headed downstairs, promising to make sure all of the kids went to sleep. It was good to have other adults in the house, just in case, and I relaxed a little.

I was still curled up next to Elora, stroking her bath-dampened hair, when I heard the garage door open. It had been a long day at work for Travis, made even longer by the MBA night classes he was taking. He came into the bedroom, slipped his loosened tie off over his head, dropped his computer bag and keys near the nightstand, and kicked off his black leather shoes. He smiled at me beneath heavy lids, dark circles around his brown eyes hinting at too many late-night study sessions.

"How're my girls?" He kissed me, then kissed Elora's cheek.

I stopped humming her favorite lullaby. "It's been a rough night." I explained how sick Elora had been.

He reached over to feel her forehead. "Do you think we

should take her to a doctor? There's probably an after-hours clinic close by."

"Maybe. There's a good chance she's dehydrated. But she's sleeping really well right now. I hope that means the worst is over."

"Well, let's watch her." Travis went to the closet to change out of his business clothes.

"How was school tonight?" I asked.

He popped his head around the corner so I could see his face. "I learned one really great thing in my accounting class. It's the only thing I'll ever need to know about accounting."

I took the bait. "Oh, yeah? What's that?"

"Someday when I own my own business, I'll be hiring an accountant."

I giggled. Beside me, Elora stirred. I froze, hoping I hadn't just woken her. But her eyes stayed closed and her breathing remained deep and slow.

Travis continued to tell me about work and school. While he talked, Elora stirred again. A small shiver, a soft moan.

A minute later, it happened again, only the sound that came from her throat was unusual, pained. I stopped listening to Travis, all my attention focused on Elora.

She looked so peaceful. Maybe I was worrying over nothing, but as I watched, a fourth, even louder moan forced its way from deep inside her chest. Her back arched, hands clenched into fists, legs and arms shaking, then stillness. Not my imagination. Something was wrong. I interrupted Travis.

"Babe!" I called him over to the bed. "Watch. She's shaking and making this weird sound."

We held our breath, waiting, my heartbeat ticking away

seconds so loudly I was sure Travis could hear them. Nothing. Elora didn't move. Travis was about to return to the closet when Elora's whole body went rigid, shaking wildly. Her throat issued that deep, painful moan again and again until I felt sure the sound of it would haunt my nightmares. And then it just stopped.

Panic surged white-hot through my chest as my mind registered a single word.

Seizure.

I jumped off the bed, frantic to rouse her. I moved her arms, shook her legs, rubbed her face and tummy. "Elora. Elora. Come on, baby. Wake up. Wake up!" Nothing. She didn't move except for the small rise and fall of her chest breathing.

I snatched her up into my arms, shocked by her limp unresponsiveness. Her head lolled backward. Hard.

"Travis! She won't wake up!" I screamed, turning to him. He had already put on his shoes and coat. He knelt by the nightstand, searching for the keys he had dropped earlier.

Footsteps pounded on the stairs, and Jared appeared in the bedroom doorway.

"I heard screaming. What's going on?" He looked at me holding Elora's limp body, frozen with fear. Travis stood, recovered keys in hand.

"Dude," Jared said to Travis, "Something's not right. You guys need to go to the hospital. Now."

Jared's declaration gave my paralyzed body permission to act. I scrambled into the closet, still holding Elora, and slipped on the first pair of shoes I could find, grabbed a jacket with my free hand, and ran to Elora's bedroom for a blanket.

Travis had already loaded baby Noah into the van and

backed out of the driveway by the time I burst through the front door like a shot. I leaped over the brown, wilted flower bed, shoes crunching on frozen grass as I ran. The sliding van door stood open, ready for me. I dove inside just as another seizure hit Elora. I held her close against my body—panic, a python around my neck as Elora convulsed in my arms, her fingers tangled in my hair.

Travis revved the engine, and the van lurched forward. I glanced out the window. Jared stood under the porch light, hands in his pockets, like a sentinel. I hadn't asked, but I knew he would care for the children we were leaving behind.

Seizure after seizure racked Elora's body as Travis sped out of our neighborhood toward the local hospital. I closed my eyes and swallowed down the panic clawing its way up my throat. All I could do was hold Elora tight and pray for green traffic lights.

"How is she?" Travis asked as he merged onto the freeway.

"I don't know. Trav, I'm so scared."

"Me too."

The hospital parking lot was nearly empty of cars. Travis drove across the painted white lines on a straight trajectory to the emergency room doors. He swerved into the parking space nearest the entrance, but even before the van came to a complete stop, I opened the door, jumped out, and started running.

The glowing red sign above the ER door called like a beacon, promising help.

Run faster. Get inside.

Travis lifted Noah in his car seat out of the van and caught up to me. The automatic doors opened upon our approach. My feet hit the waiting room carpet and I stopped to get my bearings.

I turned to the left. Rows of blessedly empty chairs.

Spinning back to the right, I spotted a woman in blue scrubs behind a glass window with a small speaking hole cut in the center.

I ran to the window.

"We need help."

"Okay, tell me what's going on," she said through the glass.

"My daughter . . . she's, uh... I think she's having seizures. She won't wake up." I bit the inside of my bottom lip to stop it from trembling. I needed to stay in control for Elora, to get her help as quickly as possible.

"What's her name?"

"Elora Isaacson."

"And you are her parents?"

Travis and I answered in unison, "Yes."

She asked more questions, typing answers calmly into her computer like we'd popped into the ER for a friendly chat. I bounced on the balls of my feet, rocking Elora side to side, barely restraining my impatience.

And then Elora had another seizure. The nurse forgot her keyboard and rose from her chair.

"Wow. Okay. Let me get you straight back to see the doctor."

Finally!

She disappeared behind the double doors leading into the ER. I paced back and forth in front of those doors, still cradling Elora, too anxious to sit down.

"Sweetheart, I'll hold her," Travis offered.

But I couldn't make myself let go. If I kept her close, I could keep her safe.

The nurse returned and ushered us into a small exam room.

"There's only one doctor in the ER tonight, but he's aware of your situation and he'll hurry in as soon as he can."

"Thank you," I said, but I wished I'd been brave enough to beg for him to hurry.

The nurse slipped Elora's medical chart into a box on the outside wall and left the door open. I stood in the doorway, willing the doctor to appear. Words of a whispered prayer poured through my silent lips. *Please, Heavenly Father, please, please help us.*

And the Lord, he it is that doth go before thee;
he will be with thee, he will not fail thee,
neither forsake thee: fear not, neither be dismayed.

DEUTERONOMY 31:8

7

GREEN STRIPED T-SHIRT

ELORA'S SEIZURES increased in severity and frequency, and still the doctor didn't come. My back and shoulders ached from holding her, but I held tight as she convulsed, her arms locked in awkward positions, fingers still tangled in my hair.

Helplessness dragged on me like an inescapable current. Tears squeezed from my eyes. With every seizure, I whispered into Elora's ear, "Hold on, baby girl. I'm right here. The doctor's coming."

Travis stood as close as possible, stroking Elora's forehead, his left arm around my waist. "Sweetheart, please. Let me take a turn."

The ache in his voice said he needed to hold her as much as I did. So, I turned and let him take Elora from me just in time for another seizure. His strong arms held her gently.

"Daddy's got you. Daddy's got you. Daddy's got you," he chanted.

The gritting of my teeth could no longer hold back the tidal wave of fear, and the dam around my courage crumbled. I sobbed.

After an eternity of seizures, the doctor finally arrived. Travis laid Elora on the hospital bed and the doctor set right to examining her, ordering tests, and prescribing a medicated IV drip that would help her relax. A nurse started the IV in Elora's hand, and within minutes, the seizures had stopped. But she still didn't wake. The doctor put a rush order on several tests and promised to return as soon as he had answers.

Travis and I stood at Elora's bedside, thankful that she could finally lay still, yet frantic to know what was going on. Why the seizures? Why couldn't she wake up?

I stroked Elora's face, begging her silently with my heart to open her eyes, fussing over her so she would know I was there—straightening her T-shirt pajamas, arranging her arms and feet more comfortably. I slipped my hand under her right cheek to adjust her head into a more natural position and noticed that the shoulder of the green-striped T-shirt where her cheek had been resting was covered in a dark red splotch.

Blood. But where was it coming from?

I lifted my hand away from Elora's face and flipped up my palm. Red-streaked saliva covered my fingers and spread across Elora's cheek.

"Trav. She's bleeding."

"What? From where?"

I showed him the stain. "Looks like her mouth."

Together, we gently separated her lips.

Elora's teeth were clamped shut like a vise. Bits of pink flesh peeked out from cracks between her molars.

"She's biting her tongue..." I said, not knowing what to do. I placed my thumbs in her mouth and tried to pry her teeth apart, gently at first, then with increasing force. But her jaw wouldn't budge. And I didn't want to hurt her.

"Where is the doctor? She needs help!" I wanted him to come and fix her.

"I'll see if I can find the nurse." Travis walked out the door.

I couldn't stand still. I paced circles around the tiny room.

Travis stepped back in. "She says she'll be in as soon as she can. They're pretty swamped out there."

"I know they are, but I can't stand this!" Tears stung my eyes as I continued to pace. But it didn't help.

"Krista, I think we could both use a distraction. Why don't we call our parents?" Travis suggested.

Barely a day passed that I didn't call my mom. If ever I needed to hear her voice, it was now, but I was worried. "It's nearly midnight. I don't want to freak them out."

"You know they'll want to know."

I dug my cell phone out of my pocket.

My mom answered, sleepy but worried. "Krista? What's wrong?"

Her voice poked holes in my defenses, and I broke down. "Mom, we're in the emergency room with Elora." Through my tears, I gave her a quick rundown of the evening while she relayed the details to my anxious father. When I'd finished, my parents poured their love through the phone, promising to pray for Elora and for us. I promised to keep them updated. I ended the call more firmly rooted. Supported.

Travis called his parents next with a similar effect.

With our courage sandbagged, we sat beside each other in metal-framed upholstered chairs watching Elora.

The nurse stepped in to check on us, and we showed her Elora's teeth and tongue. She explained that jaw clenching can happen during seizures and that trying to pry her teeth apart could actually cause more damage. The medicine calming her seizures would hopefully relax her jaw, too.

It wasn't the quick fix I'd hoped for, but I agreed to watch and see.

More waiting.

No change.

I prayed and watched and unknowingly squeezed fingernail marks into the palms of my hands.

We had waited for two agonizing hours when the doctor returned holding a manila folder, the answers we both needed and feared inside.

"The blood and urine tests point to a diagnosis of juvenile diabetes." He believed Elora's seizures were a symptom of insulin shock resulting in a diabetic coma.

I breathed out long and slow, tension melting from my muscles. Diabetes was huge and frightening and life-changing, but the diagnosis could have been much worse. Diabetes was treatable. Something we could learn to manage.

Travis and I peppered the doctor with questions. "So, she'll recover? Wake up? Will her coma cause any long-term damage? Can she live a full, active life?"

He listened patiently, then set the manila folder aside and rubbed a hand down his face. "Great questions, but I gotta tell ya, I'm just a dumb ER doctor. I know a *little* bit about a *lot* of things. I think the best option is for you to get a second opinion."

I'd never heard a doctor speak so frankly. "Okay. . ." I said. "From who?"

"I'd like to transfer Elora to Primary Children's Medical

Center. The experts there can answer your questions and start training you to take care of her."

Strangely, his honesty about his professional limitations left me confident that his suggestion was sound. This was a man who put Elora's health before his own pride. Travis and I agreed. "Sounds like a good plan."

The ambulance ride to Primary Children's Medical Center (PCMC) was quiet—lights only, no siren. Travis insisted I ride with Elora while he followed behind with Noah in the van. I sat on a small, vinyl-covered bench within reach of Elora's left hand, two EMTs riding along to monitor her. I chatted with them for a bit about their jobs and families but soon fell into silence, exhaustion giving in to the lull of the humming motor and buzzing tires.

I focused on Elora, watching her breathe. The red stain on her shoulder caught my eye. The stain would never completely wash out—I knew that. But I didn't care. If that shirt offered her any measure of comfort, if it helped her know I was close by, if it had any power to shield her from further harm, it was the smallest thing in the world to give up. I'd give Elora all I had if it would make any difference.

But it won't. I can't fix her.

Suddenly the silence was too big, and I was too alone. I sat forward and looked out the small rear windows of the ambulance, hoping for a glimpse of Travis. But he wasn't there. I took my cell phone from my pocket, but the battery was dead. I knew Travis had asked Jared to meet him off the freeway with some supplies from home, but I'd expected him to have caught up by now.

I watched and watched out the window as the miles of

highway sped away. Soon we would arrive at PCMC, and I didn't want to go in alone. It was all too much to handle on my own.

Gripping the edge of the bench with both hands, I offered a silent prayer.

Please, Heavenly Father. I don't want to be alone.

Travis had been with me from Elora's first seizure. His arrival home just moments before was too perfectly timed to be a coincidence. Without him there, I would have had to get Elora to the hospital on my own. I wondered if God had held Elora's illness off just long enough for Travis to make it home.

And then there was Jared and his family, who had arranged to stay the night at our house. Without them, who would have watched my kids? And how long would it have taken to arrange that? Another blessing too perfectly orchestrated to be a coincidence.

And what about the strong urge I'd felt to take Elora with me to my meeting instead of leaving her with Tara? And the "dumb ER doctor" who happened to be the one working at the hospital that night, who was willing to put Elora's well-being before his own pride?

These were all blessings I hadn't known I would need until that moment. But God had. And He had pre-arranged them all.

It was as if I'd come to a rocky, jagged spot on the trail of my life only to find that God had sent my brother Jesus to walk a step ahead, preparing the way, placing little cushions to ease the sharpness a bit. His way of letting me know He was there with me. Christ's grace, like a spiritual green-striped T-shirt wrapped around me by my Father in Heaven.

Not alone.

As I looked back over the night, I could see it was covered with Christ's fingerprints. I had not once been alone the entire time. And if Christ had been with me all along, placing cushions along the path before I knew I needed them, was it possible He was there still, on the path just ahead, placing more?

Yes. I had to believe that whatever lay ahead for Elora, for me, and for Travis, Christ would stay with us.

I looked out the back windows again, searching cars in the dark, straining to see through the headlights blaring in my eyes. Then a familiar silhouette, and Travis was there. He had found me. I slumped back against the ambulance wall.

Father, thank you. For getting Travis back to me. And for not leaving me on my own.

I can do all things through Christ
which strengtheneth me.

PHILLIPPIANS 4:13

8

"ALL WILL BE WELL"

THE MOMENT Elora passed through the emergency room doors at PCMC, the attending physician knew she was in trouble. He'd received word we were coming and met us at the doors, waving the EMTs to wheel Elora into a small exam room lined with unused, plastic-draped equipment. There was hardly room for me, Travis, Noah, and the four nurses who waited inside.

Three of the nurses transferred Elora from the ambulance gurney into a hospital bed. The fourth, the head nurse, offered us two folding chairs and showed us where we could stow our belongings. Travis shook the EMTs' hands as they left. Noah slept soundly in his car seat. I tucked him into the corner of the room behind us, where he would be safely out from under foot.

Nurses rushed around Elora, checking her vital signs, hooking her up to monitors and a new IV bag. Two quick knuckle raps on the half-opened door, and the doctor entered. He wore green scrubs and had a neatly trimmed goatee.

"Hello. I'm Dr. Jackson, attending physician in the ER tonight. This is Elora?"

"Yes," Travis and I answered together.

He approached Elora's bed and removed a small light from his pocket. He lifted one of Elora's eyelids and quickly moved the light across her line of sight.

"The doctor at American Fork said something about seizures? That right?"

"Yes," Travis answered. "He says she has diabetes."

He looked into Elora's other eye with the light, then opened her lips.

"She's biting her tongue," I explained.

He prodded the pink tissue between her teeth with a gloved finger. "Yes, she is." He snapped off the flashlight. "The nurses will finish getting her settled, and I'll be back in a few minutes." He turned and left as quickly as he'd come.

A receptionist scurried into the room with a stack of papers for us to sign while the head nurse asked questions about Elora's medical history. Just as we finished, a young medical student with spiky blond hair came in with a clipboard.

"I know the nurse already took Elora's medical history, but I'm here to see if you can think of any details that might help us figure out what's wrong."

"Okay," I said, wondering why they were ignoring the fact that Elora had already been diagnosed.

Travis and I mined our memories for information about my pregnancy, Elora's birth and infancy, stories of her mischievous exploits, descriptions of the tantrums she'd been throwing ever since Noah was born, and her recent surgery to remove her adenoids and tonsils. I described Elora's unsteadiness after her nap that evening, her inability to hold her sippy cup, and the night's illness and seizures.

"All right," he said, finishing his notes. "I have one last list of questions that Dr. Jackson has instructed me to ask you." The medical student slid a white piece of paper from the back of his clipboard and began reading.

"Has your child fallen recently?"

"Has your child ever had a serious head injury?"

"Does your child attend daycare?"

"Is your child ever in the care of someone who might abuse her physically?"

No, no, no, and NO!

My mind reeled. What was going on? What did any of these questions have to do with juvenile diabetes? Uneasiness pricked at my skin. My eyes shifted to Travis. His pinched eyebrows mirrored my own confusion. We answered each question with complete honesty, and then the medical student and all of the nurses left the room, leaving us in a tailspin.

"Trav, what was that all about? Why are they asking us about her head?"

"I have no idea, but I have a feeling there's something they aren't telling us."

I had the same suspicion. "Do they think we did something to her?"

"Maybe."

I blanched, horrified.

When the door opened again, Dr. Jackson entered, followed by the blond medical student and all of the nurses from before. They stood at one end of the room, the judges of an inquisition.

I straightened my back and tried to look each one in the eye. *We've done nothing wrong.* But still, my cheeks reddened under their gaze. Travis held my hand. We were in this together. Whatever *this* was.

Dr. Jackson stepped forward.

"I am going to ask you the same questions about your daughter, and I need you to answer them honestly, with any details you may have missed."

I nodded, too unsure of my voice to speak.

He held the same white sheet of paper the medical student had used.

"Has your child fallen recently?"

"No."

"Has your child ever had a serious head injury?"

"No."

"Does your child attend daycare?"

"No."

"Is your child ever in the care of someone who might abuse her physically?"

"Heavens, no."

"The notes here say you've noticed some shakiness lately. Tell me about that."

I related once more how Elora had stumbled into the kitchen while I cooked grilled cheese sandwiches. How her hands shook as she reached for her sippy cup.

"And what about these tantrums she's been throwing?"

The tantrums began shortly after Noah was born. For no apparent reason, Elora would burst into fits—screaming, crying, flailing around on the floor. Sometimes she would rub her hands or feet together or push her forehead across the carpet. She always refused to let me touch her or comfort her. And I would end up in tears myself, wishing I knew how to help her.

For an entire month, I'd blamed the tantrums on the "terrible twos" and jealousy over the new baby, but as weeks passed with no letup, I took her to the pediatrician to search for another answer. His examination revealed that Elora's large tonsils and adenoids were obstructing her breathing and probably disrupting her sleep. Better sleep would equal fewer tantrums. An operation was scheduled for Halloween Day. It had now been three months since Elora's operation. Her sleeping had indeed improved, but her tantrums had not.

The look on Dr. Jackson's face told me that Travis and I had confirmed whatever suspicions he was hiding. He took one more step forward and spoke in a voice filled with urgency.

"Your daughter is a *very* sick little girl. And you have every right to be *very* worried about her."

Tears flooded my vision. Travis asked, "What's wrong with her?"

With a nod of his head, Dr. Jackson signaled to his team, and they all jumped into motion. "We need to take her right away for a CT scan of her head." He was not asking our permission.

The nurses and medical student swarmed around Elora. Travis and I rose to our feet. Dr. Jackson propped open the door as the nurses wheeled Elora's bed out of the room.

Pointing at Travis, he ordered, "Dad, come with me."

Then to me, "Mom, stay here with baby."

A rush of bodies and equipment. Then everyone was gone.

I was left in silence—alone and accused.

No. Not alone.

There was Christ.

And Noah.

I retrieved the car seat from the corner behind me and peered beneath his blanket. Still sleeping soundly.

I should let him sleep.

But my frightened heart and empty arms quickly won the debate. I lifted him from the warm confines of the car seat. He stretched, arching his back, tucking his legs beneath him. I nuzzled my nose behind his downy ear and inhaled his sweet newborn scent.

He opened his eyes. They were turning brown like Travis's. He focused on my face. Recognition. Then a little toothless grin. That smile, naïve to the trouble surrounding us, lightened my heart. I kissed his cheek.

"I love you too, little man."

I tried to track how long Travis and Elora had been gone, but every time I looked at the clock, my distraught mind forgot what time it had been the last time I looked. Minutes passed like hours. I played with Noah and nursed him, and eventually, someone came back for me. A nurse with a kind face.

"Elora's scan is finished, and she's being admitted to the hospital. Your husband is with her. I'll help you carry your things and take you to them if you're ready."

"I'd love that."

Something had shifted. The air of suspicion had deflated from the room.

Why? Had Elora's CT scan absolved us of blame?

I slung the diaper bag over one shoulder and wrapped Noah's blanket tightly around him. The nurse picked up the car seat, our coats, and Travis's computer bag.

She led me down a corridor to the elevator, up a couple of floors, and down a hallway into a large green room strongly scented with antiseptic. Travis met me at the door with a kiss. He took Noah from me.

"Are you all right? What happened?" I asked him. "No one

ever came back to tell me anything."

"I'm fine. I was with Elora the whole time. As soon as the CT scan was finished, they brought us here, and I asked one of the nurses to find you."

I gave him a long hug, and when I pulled away, Travis gestured to the far side of the room. "There's your girl."

I walked briskly to her, my shoes squeaking on the shiny tiled floor. Separation had been a rubber band stretched too tightly between us.

Two nurses standing on either side of Elora's bed greeted me with warm smiles. I watched them—checking the beeping monitors, straightening wires and tubes, taping and retaping so everything would stay where it was supposed to be on Elora's body. They worked free of the urgency and suspicion from before. Again, I wondered what had changed.

"How is she?" I asked generally to everyone in the room.

The nurse who had escorted me to the room spoke first. "Dr. Jackson wants to spend some time with you both to discuss the results of Elora's CT scan. He's making sure everything is resolved with his other patients so he can give you his full attention. He'll be in as soon as he's finished." She left to attend to other duties, closing the door behind her.

Her words were meant to set us at ease, and they would have if my motherly instincts hadn't stood on end. The doctor's delay. His need to finish with his other patients...

Do emergency room doctors normally give their "full attention" to cases that aren't serious?

Travis walked the floor, bouncing and cooing to Noah while I stood above Elora's head stroking her cheeks, cautious of the oxygen tube freshly taped beneath her nose. I leaned down and kissed her forehead. As I stood back up, something by my left hand caught my eye. Green-striped fabric with a blood stain at one edge folded neatly beside Elora's pillow. I'd been so excited to see her, I hadn't noticed that she'd been changed into a small blue hospital gown with a logo where the green striped pocket had been.

Replaced.

With a swift hand, I snatched the shirt and stuffed it into the diaper bag still slung over my shoulder before anyone could see how much it hurt me to put it away.

I should have expected it. Did I really think they were going to leave her in that old blood-soaked shirt? But it had been meant to keep her safe, continuously wrapped in a piece of me even when I wasn't at her side. My heart fell into a field of nettles.

"Your little girl is beautiful," one of the nurses said.

I nodded, but kept my head down to hide the hurt flush that had crept into my cheeks.

"Look how long her hair is!" the other nurse gushed.

"And those eyelashes!"

I couldn't help it. I smiled.

"What is she like?"

I struggled to find the right words, my insides a spaghetti bowl.

"She's absolute mischief." I laughed through my tears.

Both nurses smiled.

They asked questions about her, and once I started talking, I couldn't stop. I told them everything. What foods she liked, her best-loved toys, favorite Winnie the Pooh shoes. The shows she watched over and over, the books we read before bed, silly games she played in the car. The way she sucked the two middle fingers on her left hand so it looked like she was always saying "I love you" in sign language, only she said it like "I luz you" instead. The story of how she'd buzzed her hair, and how long it had taken to grow out her bangs. Travis sat nearby, wiping his eyes.

It was the perfect therapy session. The nurses listened, laughed, and cried. And by the time I couldn't think of anything else to say, I knew they truly cared about Elora—and me.

They finished making Elora as comfortable as possible, and then left the room to give us some alone time with our girl.

Travis carried two folding chairs across the floor next to the bed. We sat facing each other, leaning forward, clasping hands. I knew we needed to talk, to prepare for what was coming. But I had no idea how.

Travis was the one who broke the silence. "I think the doctor is bringing us bad news."

"I know."

"Are you going to be okay?"

"I hope so."

Silence again.

I squeezed Travis's hand. "How about you? Will you be okay?"

"I'd like to give Elora a blessing. Would you like one too?"

I did not hesitate. "Yes."

Travis slipped out to the hall and found a male nurse, also a member of our faith, who could assist with the blessings. The nurse anointed Elora's head with oil consecrated for the healing of the sick, then he and Travis placed their hands on the top of her head while Travis spoke the blessing.

Travis asked God to protect her and heal her, according to His will and plan.

He blessed Elora to be free from pain.

And he prayed that even in her coma, she would know that her parents were nearby and loved her.

My tears flowed freely through the blessing.

Then it was my turn.

I sat in a chair, and both men stood behind me. They placed their hands on my head, and Travis once again spoke the blessing.

He blessed me with strength to endure the challenges ahead.

That I would know there were loved ones here and in heaven praying for me right now.

And finally, a promise from God that "All will be well."

With the blessing finished, I stood, shook the nurse's hand, and thanked him for coming.

He left quietly.

Travis and I sat once more in the folding chairs at Elora's bedside.

I wiped my eyes and blew my nose, the words of the blessing filling my heart with helium hope.

"What are you thinking?" Travis asked.

I smiled. "In the blessing, Heavenly Father said that 'all will be well.'"

"Yes."

"Honey, I think He's telling us Elora's going to be okay!" I started to cry again, but this time from sheer joy and relief.

But Travis just stared at the floor.

"Trav, what is it? Tell me."

"It's just... what if it means something else?"

"No." I wanted him to stop talking. I was right. I knew I was. I *had* to be.

"Krista...listen."

"I don't want it to mean anything else."

"I know. I don't either." He rubbed the top of my hand with his thumb. His eyes were red from crying, and the lines in his forehead and cheeks were deeper than I'd ever seen them. He was as sick with worry as I was.

My heart softened. "I'm sorry, babe. I just want everything to be okay."

Travis nodded. "But that's exactly what I think God is trying to say. That no matter what happens—good or bad—all will *eventually* be well. He'll help us through whatever is coming. And we really will be okay. I feel it, honey. I really do."

I scooted to the edge of my chair, put my arms around his shoulders, and buried my face in his neck. He tucked my hair behind my ear and stroked my cheek.

"I know you do," I mumbled into his skin, "but is it okay if I still pray for a miracle?"

"Of course. That's what I'll be praying for too."

I kissed his cheek, then retook my position at the head of Elora's bed. Travis bumped me playfully with his hip until I made room for him to stand beside me. We leaned against each other, staring down at our daughter, lost in private thought.

The words "all will be well" played on repeat in my head. Travis was right. God hadn't promised anything except hope for the future. I still held on to my faith that Elora would recover and life would go back to normal, but I had to admit that no matter what happened, there was comfort in knowing that God could see days ahead for me dawning bright and beautiful. I only had one wish.

Please, Father, let Elora be a part of those days.

And this is the confidence that we have in him,
that, if we ask any thing according to his will,
he heareth us.

1 JOHN 5:14

9

TONSILS

THE SUDDEN CLICK of the metallic door handle made me jump, resurfacing my thoughts from the depths of my meditation. It was Dr. Jackson.

"Thank you for your patience. I wanted to make sure we'd have plenty of time to talk, but it took longer than I thought to wrap everything up with my other patients."

This was not the same man who'd greeted us with suspicion when we arrived at the hospital. It occurred to me that in his profession, he must witness the worst of human behavior, and though it was frightening to be accused of abuse, those protocols were in place for a reason. He'd just been doing his job.

Dr. Jackson held the door open and another doctor, also wearing green scrubs, followed him into the room. "This is my colleague, Dr. Duhon. I've asked him to join us." He was fit and tan, ash-blond curls falling from the back of his scrub hat, the white face mask dangling from his neck suggesting he'd come straight from surgery to speak with us. Travis and I shook his hand.

Both doctors grabbed folding chairs from a stack near the door and carried them across the green floor to join us near

Elora. I sat beside Travis, trying to look brave as my insides turned to overcooked oatmeal.

All will be well. All will be well...

Dr. Jackson began, "I've never found an easy way to deliver hard news to parents. I think it's best just to come right out and say it."

Hard news? I'd thought I was ready. I wasn't. My body tensed, bracing for the hit as the doctor pulled a folded piece of white printer paper from his front shirt pocket.

"These are Elora's CT scan results."

He unfolded the paper and held it out in front of us. Travis and I looked down onto a black-and-white printout of Elora's brain, but before I could reason out what I was seeing, the doctor dropped his bomb.

"She has a brain tumor."

The words struck with a concussive force that tore the air from my lungs and burned my skin. I fumbled for Travis's hand at the same time he reached for mine. Our fingers intertwined in a frantic grasp to find something solid to hold on to.

No, no, no, no... This was supposed to be diabetes! They were gonna wake her up! We were gonna take her home! Oh, please, not Elora. Please.

I sucked oxygen faster and deeper into my lungs—tingling numbness spreading through my fingers, my nose, my lips.

My mind turned hazy, distant. Reality, a show I watched on a screen. CT scans. Brain tumors. Those were words you heard on the news or in hospital dramas. Happening to someone else. Not in real life. Not in my life.

Dr. Jackson took the cap off a pen and used it to point at a dark splotch in the center of the left side of Elora's brain.

"This is a fluid-filled cyst, and we believe the tumor is underneath. It's in a difficult spot, with healthy brain tissue surrounding it on all sides. Normally, the brain looks something like this." He flipped the paper over and drew a rudimentary sketch.

"Each half of the brain has a small crescent-shaped space in the center that holds cerebrospinal fluid. Excess fluid drains from the brain down through the spinal cord." Flipping the page again, he pointed at the dark tumor splotch.

"Elora's tumor has blocked the drain of excess fluid." He then pointed to the right side of Elora's brain. The space in the center bore no resemblance to the small crescent shape he had drawn. Instead, it looked like a large misshapen swimming pool.

"Excess fluid is collecting on both sides of her brain. This condition is called hydrocephalus. It's creating a lot of pressure and swelling inside her brain. It's why she's having seizures, and it's why she can't wake up."

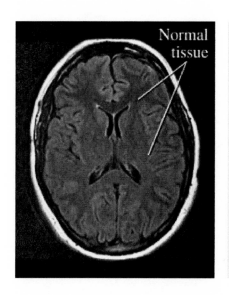 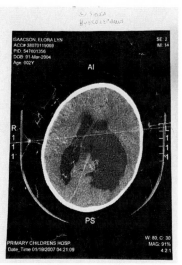

Image of a healthy brain compared to Elora's CT scan
January 19, 2007

Several moments of stunned silence passed while the doctors allowed us time to process. I pressed my fist hard into my cheek to prove to myself I was awake, to force my lungs to remember to breathe, but my mind struggled to keep up, dragging this new information through a thick, muddy swamp of shock.

Don't you fall apart. If you fall apart, these doctors are going to have to take care of you, and that will take time away from Elora.

I turned around in my chair to look at Elora's perfect, beautiful face, my heart aching for the pain she was in. I hadn't seen it. I hadn't helped her. "How long has it been there? The tumor," I asked Dr. Jackson.

"I think this is a fast-growing, childhood onset tumor, which means Elora has probably had it since she was a newborn, if not before."

I looked at Travis, then back at the doctor, mortified. "Her whole life? The whole time?"

"Probably."

Travis shook his head. "Then why didn't we notice any symptoms?"

"Or...did I miss something?" I blurted out before the horror of the idea could stop my mouth.

What if I missed something? What if this is all my fault?

Something deep inside snapped, a broken thread pulled, unraveling every stitch of my motherly confidence.

"Mrs. Isaacson, you didn't miss anything." But Dr. Jackson must have sensed my skepticism because he leaned forward and looked into my eyes. "I promise."

I shook my head. That wasn't possible. *I'm her mother. I should have known.*

"From what you've told me, the only symptom she exhibited is what we call Drunken Sailor Syndrome. People with brain tumors will sometimes exhibit shaking, unsteadiness, a lack of coordination. This symptom is not necessarily indicative of a tumor, but once a tumor is discovered, this syndrome is found to be a common side effect. In a toddler, these symptoms are easily overlooked because children are naturally unsteady. You wouldn't have suspected."

I still didn't believe him.

"Honestly..." Dr. Jackson sighed. "Even if you'd brought her in weeks ago, this tumor is so aggressive, it probably wouldn't have made much difference."

Travis asked, "So, what do we do? Is it treatable?"

"That's why I've asked Dr. Duhon to join us. He's a pediatric neurosurgeon, and he's here to discuss treatment options with you."

Dr. Duhon had remained quiet throughout the conversation. But now Travis and I looked to him for all the answers. His voice was calm, but confident.

"The first thing we need to do is place a shunt in Elora's head to drain off some of the fluid and relieve the pressure. Once we do that, we'll be able to do an MRI, which is a much better scan to determine exactly where the tumor is, how big it is, and the best way to treat it, but we'll probably start radiation and chemotherapy by the end of the day."

By the end of the day?

Everything was happening so fast. I wanted to call a time-out, step aside, and think for a minute. But time was something Elora couldn't afford.

Dr. Duhon continued, "With Elora in such critical

condition, I'd like to get things moving right away. Unless you have any questions."

Travis and I both shook our heads.

"Then I'll go get everything prepped for the procedure, and I'll be back for Elora when we're ready."

We all four stood at the same time. Dr. Duhon headed right for the door. Dr. Jackson shook our hands. "I'm so sorry. This is something no parent should have to face. I'll be checking on Elora's progress, and I hope everything goes smoothly."

"Thank you," I said numbly.

The moment the door closed behind him, I released the choke hold on my heart. I rushed to Elora, held her face in my hands, and sobbed openly.

"Baby girl, I'm so, so sorry. I'm sorry that you've been hurting so badly. I'm sorry I didn't know. I didn't know!" My heart tore itself to shreds.

Travis stood by me, holding Elora's hand, tears flowing.

"Trav, what are we gonna do?"

"I don't know." He wiped his face with the back of his hand. "But I think we should call our parents and have them spread the word. We need prayers."

I dialed the number and woke my parents again. "Dad... it's a brain tumor. I'm so scared!" It was all I could get out. My body shook uncontrollably and I wailed so hard, there was barely room left in my throat for sound.

Mom jumped on the call. "Sweetheart, I'm packing my things and getting in the car. I'm coming to you right now." Dad would follow as soon as he could arrange things at the granite shop.

I cried hard into the back of my hand, but managed to say,

"Be safe. Hurry." I knew I wouldn't relax while she covered the 400 miles from Boise to Salt Lake City in the dark alone.

"I'm coming, honey. Hold on."

Thankfully, both sets of Travis's parents lived nearby. His mother, Kathy, also told us she was on her way. While Travis called his dad and stepmom, I stood beside Elora, desperate for her to open her eyes so I could look into them and ask for her forgiveness.

Why didn't I see she was so sick? Why didn't I get her help? Weren't mothers supposed to have instincts or premonitions about things like this?

My tears wet her forehead and fell into her hair while mountainous rockslides of guilt crashed over me.

I should have protected her!

Remorse bulged and swelled, smothering me beneath its weight. I clung to the sides of her bed, sucking in great gasps of air between throat-tearing sobs. It was too heavy. Crushing me. I couldn't get out.

Squeezing my eyes shut, I sent a one-word prayer heavenward.

Help!

God was the only one who could.

A seemingly random memory flittered to the surface of my mind.

Another hospital. Halloween day. Elora in a different blue hospital gown, fuzzy yellow socks, hair in braids.

Elora's tonsil surgery? I swiped at the memory like a fist through smoke, trying to blow it away to make room for God's help. But the memory remained.

One last kiss before surgery. Waiting room chairs. The doctor telling us the surgery went perfectly.

Elora's tonsils. What about them?

Elora waking up from anesthesia. Crying angrily. Sips of apple juice. Play-Doh and movies. Nurses and doctors checking in through that whole fitful night.

Wait. A connection. *Doctors. Nurses. Medical professionals.*

Elora had been surrounded by them for twenty-four hours. They had looked in her eyes, her ears. Listened to her heart. Taken her blood pressure. Put her under anesthesia and watched her wake up. Less than three months ago.

And no one saw anything that made them suspicious.

A bright hope rose golden over the mountain of my guilt.

If they hadn't noticed any symptoms of a tumor, maybe I really didn't miss anything!

The overwhelming reservoir of personal agony began to drain away. A slow, steady stream as I breathed. In. Out. Calming breaths.

Not my fault. No one else saw it either.

Dr. Duhon walked into the room. "We're ready."

10

PRESSURE

TRAVIS AND I EACH HELD one of Elora's hands while the nurses prepared to move her into surgery. They transferred her IV bag to a pole attached to the bed, unhooked the tubes and wires from the monitors and oxygen machine, and coiled them next to her on the mattress.

She's in good hands. They'll take care of her.

But my heart rebelled. Elora was headed into the fight for her life, and I would be forced to stay behind. I wanted to snatch her off the bed, run away, take her home. But if Elora was ever going to come home, we would have to move forward, through the battle.

A nurse released the wheel brakes on the bed. "Okay, Mom and Dad. It's time."

I kissed her hand and took one last look at her face. So still. I longed for a twitch. A flutter. A jerk. Something to tell me she was in there trying to come back to me.

Nothing.

Travis kissed her forehead. "Do good, little one."

The nurses pushed the bed toward the door held open by Dr. Duhon.

"Please take care of her," I called after them, immediately regretting the insinuation that they would do anything less.

"We will," one nurse answered, smiling.

Before he left, Dr. Duhon told us, "The OR waiting room is right down—" He leaned out the door and looked both ways, but pointed left. "That way. When the procedure is over, that's where I'll come find you. Should be about an hour, hour and a half."

He let the door swing closed. Elora was gone. I stood in the middle of the floor, worry consuming me so completely that I barely registered the impatient squeaks coming from the car seat in the corner. Noah was hungry.

Travis lifted the baby out of his seat and passed him to me. "Why don't we go downstairs to the cafeteria?"

"I'm not really hungry."

"Me neither, but we should eat something anyway. While we have a chance."

I sighed. *Better now than pulling myself away from Elora later.*

Travis loaded himself up like a pack mule, and I followed him to the elevator. Noah fussed. I bounced and rocked and gave him my knuckle to suck on.

We passed by the crowded waiting room and rode the elevator down to the hospital lobby, a brightly decorated area with giant plastic fish floating from clear wire through a forest of seaweed. The main floor of the hospital appeared deserted. Not many people coming and going during the wee hours of the morning. Travis led the way across the lobby, our footsteps echoing up through the vaulted ceiling. We stopped beneath the wide arched entrance to the cafeteria staring at our options— made-to-order omelets, a la carte muffins and pastries, fruit bowls, bagels, and juice. But nothing looked appetizing. Noah howled with impatience.

"How 'bout you sit and feed the baby. I'll get us something," Travis said.

"Sounds good." I was happy not to have to choose.

I walked to a table on the far side of the room. Travis dumped our things on the floor by my feet, then headed back toward the food counter.

While Noah nursed, the adrenaline that had kept me going through the sleepless night seeped from my blood. I propped my elbow on the table to support my head and closed my eyes. Travis returned a few minutes later with a red plastic cafeteria tray. It took several blinks to coax my eyelids into staying open.

The food was simple, but he'd chosen some things he knew I liked. "Thanks, babe," I said. I peeled a banana and took the top off a blueberry muffin. Travis speared a piece of cantaloupe from a shallow white dish.

I ate mechanically, dutifully, stress stripping the food of taste and comfort. Every bite was chewed and chewed until I could force my throat to swallow. It was a meager meal at best, but I was incapable of finishing it. Travis ate a few more bites while Noah babbled and played happily in my lap with a set of plastic keys.

Now that my stomach registered full, all my body wanted was sleep. "Babe, I saw some padded benches out in a corner of the lobby. When you're finished, it looks like a good place to lie down for a few minutes. Way quieter than the waiting room."

"Sounds good to me." Travis hauled our things to a secluded L-shaped bench covered in bubblegum-pink vinyl cushions. I rocked Noah to sleep while Travis plugged in our cell phones to charge.

With Noah snuggled back in his car seat, Travis and I stretched out on the bench, our feet touching in the corner of the L. I closed my eyes, but the quiet gave my brain too much space to run, and I kept returning to the surgical room where I was not allowed.

Movement by my feet. Travis rustling through his bag. The click of his laptop opening.

I opened my eyes. "Can't sleep either?"

"Nope. I'm gonna email my boss and let him know I'm not coming in today. Then I'll go find out how Elora is doing."

"Want me to come with you?"

"No. You and Noah stay here and rest as much as you can. I'll come back as soon as I know anything."

"I want to be there when the doctor comes to talk to us."

"I promise I'll be right back." He sent his email, then brushed my cheek with his fingers on his way to the elevator.

I tented a blanket over the car seat and rested an arm over the handle to keep Noah safe, then closed my eyes again, instructing my brain not to open them until Travis returned. Knowing he'd gone for answers helped me relax, and I drifted off. But a short time later, Travis whispered my name and I bolted upright, trying to remember where I was.

"Whoa, honey. It's okay." Travis put his hand on my shoulder.

I put my own hand over my heart and tried to slow my breathing. "Sorry. I must be stressed."

"Yeah." Travis chuckled. "I get that."

I stood and stretched and yawned, sleep sticking to me like a burr. "What'd you find out?"

"She's doing well. The surgery should be done in about twenty minutes."

"That's good. Let's get up there, then, so we don't miss the doctor."

We rode the elevator and walked down the hall toward the OR waiting room, but before we'd reached the doors, someone called out our names. We looked over our shoulders as Travis's mom and newly returned missionary brother stepped off the elevator. We hurried toward them, embracing in a tearful group hug. Their presence lifted a portion of weight from my shoulders, a pair of fresh, strong arms to help carry the load. "I've never been so glad to see a familiar face in my whole life," I said.

"How is Elora?" Kathy asked as she dug through her large purse for a tissue.

Travis explained the shunt procedure the surgeon had just performed. "He should be here any minute to talk to us, and then we'll decide where to go from there."

We found four empty seats right by the door of the crowded waiting room. Kathy took a thick skein of variegated orange yarn and a crochet hook from her bag. In less than a minute, she had a good start on a new dishcloth. McKay retold the mission stories Travis had missed at the homecoming party the night before. I chatted and listened and tried not to worry.

We only waited fifteen minutes for Dr. Duhon. Travis introduced McKay and his mom, then the doctor motioned to a glass door on the opposite wall. "Why don't we use one of the conference rooms so we can talk more privately?"

Concern slithered up my spine. Was privacy for good news or bad?

There were only two chairs in the tiny room. Kathy and I sat, Travis and McKay standing behind us. The doctor stood facing us, his back to the glass door.

"First off, the procedure went well."

Good news. Travis put his hands on my shoulders and squeezed.

"But during the surgery, Elora was having a hard time breathing on her own, so I made the decision to intubate her."

"What does that mean?" I asked.

"It means that we put a tube down into her lungs, and a ventilator machine is breathing for her right now."

The four of us muttered over one another. "But is she okay?" Travis asked.

"She's stable. The breathing tube means she won't have to work so hard to breathe. It will allow her body to focus more energy on healing. For now, the shunt is doing its job, draining off the excess spinal fluid and relieving the pressure in her brain. But that's what I wanted to talk to you about." Dr. Duhon paused and leaned back against the metal door frame, giving himself a second to find the right words.

Something's not right. My heart picked up speed.

The doctor rubbed his hands together and dove in. "Okay… so, the shunt has two main functions. It doesn't only drain fluid—it also has a gauge that measures pressure. Normal pressure in a child's brain is between ten and fifteen millimeters mercury. You need to know that when I inserted Elora's shunt, the pressure in her brain measured 135."

We all gasped. Travis's hands tightened on my shoulders as I started to cry, unable to comprehend the level of pain Elora had endured over the last few weeks. Images of her recent tantrums popped into my mind. Her screaming, crying inconsolably, refusing to let me touch her. Pressing her head into the floor. It wasn't jealousy, or tonsils, or terrible twos.

It was pain.

Unimaginable pain.

Kathy reached into my lap and held my hand, offering me a tissue.

The doctor continued, "It's the highest level of pressure I've ever seen, or in fact, ever heard of in a living person, let alone a child who was running around yesterday. Did you say you were at the airport?"

"Yes," I said. "She was riding the escalators with her cousins, eating treats at Grandma's house. She didn't even act sick until late last night."

"Honestly, I don't see how that's possible. She shouldn't be alive. It's...I don't know. This just doesn't happen."

He looked at me as if I held the secret.

But God hadn't shared the answer with me either. Considering what we just learned from the doctor, Elora should have been sick her whole life, should have spent months or years in and out of hospital beds. She should have shown symptoms long before today. But no one had recognized her pain for what it was. Not me, not Travis, not any other family members or friends or doctors. Against all medical reason and probability, her health had been preserved until this moment. To me, that left only one explanation.

I wiped my face with the tissue and looked into the doctor's eyes. "It's possible because this is God's plan for Elora."

Dr. Duhon nodded twice, and the warmth in my heart told me I was right.

Trust in the Lord with all thine heart; and lean not unto thine own understanding. In all thy ways acknowledge him, and he shall direct thy paths.

PROVERBS 3:5–6

11

CHAIN REACTION

ITH ELORA'S SHUNT successfully in place, it was time for the next step of her treatment. Dr. Duhon had ordered an MRI—a detailed scan of her brain that would pinpoint the exact dimensions and location of the tumor and help the doctors decide how to treat it. There was only an hour before the MRI appointment, and I wanted to see my girl.

Kathy and McKay kindly insisted on caring for Noah in the waiting room so Travis and I could focus on our visit with Elora. Dr. Duhon escorted us to her recovery room, but stopped us in the hallway.

"Before you see Elora, I want to prepare you."

Prepare us? To see our child?

Motherly instinct drew me toward Elora like a magnet. There was no imaginable situation where I would choose to stay away. But the concern on the doctor's face hinted that not every parent he'd accompanied had been as strong as they hoped. I reined in my impatience and listened.

"Elora is attached to several monitors, the new intubation tube is taped to her face, and the cranial shunt I inserted is visible so you'll be able to see the fluid draining. Be prepared for that."

So far, there was nothing I hadn't already anticipated, but I gulped down the information, hoping to inoculate myself against falling apart.

"The machines in the room are noisy, but they're all important," Dr. Duhon continued. "The ventilator and shunt monitor, there's a heart monitor, a blood pressure monitor, and a couple of others. But the nurses will take care of all that. The main thing that you need to be aware of is the intubation tube. If it gets dislodged, it might not be possible to get it back in. And that could cause complications."

The seriousness of his warning was not lost on me. I bobbed my head up and down. A slideshow of images flipped through my mind. Elora smiling. Elora laughing. Elora playing dress-up, running, wrestling with her brothers, sucking her fingers, coloring with Shaustia, dancing in the kitchen. Would she be able to do those things again? What if the treatments to remove the tumor damaged parts of her brain so she couldn't walk, or talk, or smile? What side effects would chemo and radiation have? Would she lose her hearing? Her sight?

Stop! Don't think about it.

I would wait for the doctors to decide the best treatment options for Elora, and then I would ask my questions. Not before. Not now. It was too hard. I just wanted to be back at her side, smothering her with kisses. Everything else could wait.

"Do you have any questions?" Dr. Duhon asked.

I quieted the voices in my head before answering, "No."

The doctor reached for the handle of the door. "Ready?"

Travis peered down at me with raised eyebrows, checking on my state of mind and heart.

I stared at the wooden door in front of me, trying to piece together a mental picture of what awaited on the other side. Elora was in there. That's all that mattered.

"Yes. I'm ready," I told them both.

Dr. Duhon opened the door. "Then let's go in."

Travis placed his hand on the small of my back and guided me through the doorway ahead of him.

I saw the machines first, lining the entire wall to my left. Beeping, whirring, whooshing.

Four nurses, three women and one man, dressed in scrubs with kid-friendly patterns, attended to the machines, focusing on clipboard charts, wires, tubes, and IV bags. They looked up briefly from their work and greeted me with compassionate eyes and gentle smiles, the atmosphere in the room reverent with respect for our difficult situation.

I rounded the door, eyes drawn toward the foot of a metal hospital bed with a thick white cotton blanket smoothed neatly over the mattress.

A couple more steps into the room, and finally, there she was. Elora's form, so tiny in the huge bed, as still as before, the blanket tucked neatly around her chest and under her arms, IV line still taped to her left hand. The intubation tube was held in place with tape that pulled at her lips and cheeks so she didn't quite look like herself. Dr. Duhon had been right to warn me. It was harder to see her like that than I'd expected.

The nurses stopped working as I approached the bed and laid my hand on Elora's leg, gifting me a moment of dignified stillness. But the sudden attention unnerved me.

This is your girl. Just be her mama.

I leaned forward and peered at top of her head, the incision, and the drain. The entire room held its breath, waiting to see how I would react. I opened my mouth, and...

Laughed.

The sound was so unexpected, everyone in the room flinched as if I had screamed.

As my laughter continued, the nurses side-eyed one another, unsure how to react.

Turning to Travis, laughter tears rolling down my face, I squeaked out two words. "Her hair!"

He stepped around me, closer to Elora, until he could see what I had seen, the confusion on his face melting. Then he smiled and said, "Honey, you'd better explain what's going on before one of these nice people calls the psychiatric ward and has you admitted."

I sobered right up.

"I'm *so* sorry. It's just that six months ago, Elora got ahold of the hair clippers and buzzed the top of her head..." I pointed at Elora and the freshly shaved spot where the neurosurgeon had placed the shunt. "...just like that! For six months, I've been trying to grow her hair back out. I've had to hide it under hats and headbands, and it was just starting to look halfway decent, but you guys went and buzzed it right off again!"

I couldn't hold the laughter back anymore, but this time, four kind nurses joined in. The somber mood in the room evaporated, and the glow of a happy memory filled the space with warmth. Sweet and delicious to my parched soul, I drank the happiness greedily.

The nurses returned to their work, and Dr. Duhon busied himself by moving two chairs to the head of Elora's bed so Travis and I could sit near her.

"Mr. and Mrs. Isaacson, my shift is ending soon, so I'll be

turning you over to one of my colleagues. He'll be in to meet you when it's time for Elora's MRI, but if there's anything else you need before that, I'm leaving you in extremely good hands." Dr. Duhon gestured at the nurses, who waved him off with mock modesty.

"I'll be following Elora's progress, and I'll stop in tomorrow to check on her during my shift."

"Thank you," I said.

For the next hour, I laser-focused on Elora. Travis and I leaned our elbows on the edge of the mattress, drawing ourselves as close to her as possible. Elora's hand looked so tiny cupped in mine. I rubbed the calluses on her ring and middle fingers where her front teeth rested when she sucked them. Flecks of peachy nail polish stuck stubbornly to all of her other fingers, but those two nails had been sucked clean.

I pressed the back of her hand to my cheek, remembering the day six months ago that had sparked my laughter. The words, so clear in my mind after discovering her cut hair—*She loves you. She trusts you. Don't ruin that.*

What if I had ignored that prompting and cried instead, or worse, yelled at her?

My heart cringed.

I would have walked into this room and seen her hair like that, and it would have crushed me.

God had prompted me to laugh. And in that laughter, He had saved me despair in a moment that only He knew was coming. He had foreseen how my reaction then would ripple forward and taint the lens of this one. Laughter then had allowed me laughter now.

In my mind, I sent my Heavenly Father a hug.

. . . I will go before your face.
I will be on your right hand and on your left,
and my Spirit shall be in your hearts,
and mine angels round about you, to bear you up.

DOCTRINE AND COVENANTS 84:88

12

ANGELS

THE NEW NEUROSURGEON, Dr. Brockmeyer, introduced himself with a generous grin and a firm handshake. He was tall and thin, with straight sandy hair and an air of joviality that I was sure came out in spades under different circumstances. I liked him immediately.

But I wasn't ready to let Elora go. Sitting peacefully at her side had been like a deep-tissue massage for my soul, and I wasn't ready for it to be over. This pattern of coming and going played on my nerves. Stretched apart, pushed together, stretched apart like an accordion. Tight with worry, deflated with relief, on repeat.

"This won't take long," the doctor said. "About forty-five minutes for the MRI."

At least this separation would be brief and much less stressful.

The nurses began unhooking Elora from her monitors so she could be moved. Travis and I were in their way, holding Elora's hands, but we didn't budge. They worked around us like they'd taken classes on the subject, and I loved them for their understanding.

Dr. Brockmeyer and two nurses wheeled Elora from the room. Another nurse showed us the way back to the surgical waiting area to pick up Kathy, McKay, and baby Noah. After her MRI, Elora would be admitted to the Pediatric Intensive Care Unit, and there was a special waiting room for families and friends of those patients. This waiting room would be the home base for us and our visitors as long as Elora was in the PICU.

The nurse guided us into a large, dark room with a fish tank in the center like a nightlight casting a blue glow over silk potted plants, magazine racks, framed landscape art, and clusters of cream-colored vinyl chairs and couches. The PICU waiting room was kept dark throughout the night to make it comfortable for anyone attempting to sleep. For now, we were alone.

The four of us chose a comfortable-looking corner with a couch and several chairs facing each other. A spot to unload and settle down long-term. I plopped myself in the middle of the couch and propped my legs up on a chair. Kathy handed me the baby. I kissed and smooshed his little face until I'd had my fill.

Travis fell asleep next to me almost instantly, vibrating the seat with snores. Kathy and McKay chatted quietly in chairs to my right. The tropical fish swam lazily in their tank, weaving through orange coral, striped seaweed, and a sunken pirate ship. Completely at peace. Not a care in the world.

Lucky.

My eyes grew heavy as I followed the swirling patterns of their delicate fins.

Everything is going to be okay. The doctors will find the best treatment for Elora. Her shunt is working. Dr. Duhon says she's out of immediate danger. Travis is here, and Mom and McKay. I have Noah. We have a comfy spot to rest. Everything is going to be okay.

Noah slept on my chest, so I closed my eyes and let all of the tension in my body seep into the cushion beneath me, drifting toward sleep until the click of the door opening, a shaft of yellow light, and whispered voices drew me back.

"Is that her?"

"I don't know. I can't see."

I opened my eyes. Two women, their silhouettes black in the bright doorway. I squinted. The women let the door close and took a tentative step into the room. In the blue glow, I recognized their faces.

"Aunt Janice? Emily?"

My aunt and cousin rushed to me and wrapped me in a tight hug. With the first early rays of the sun, word of Elora had begun to spread.

"How did you know where to find me?" I asked.

Emily answered, "I lived in this waiting room when Hudson was here. I figured it was the best place to try first."

Emily's son Hudson, who was about the same age as Elora, had been diagnosed with an inoperable brain stem tumor just one year earlier. His chemo and radiation treatments were ongoing. Of course Emily would be one of the first to come. I hugged her again.

Janice rubbed my arm. "I just talked to your mom. She's still doing well, but wishing the drive wasn't so long."

"Thank you." I hadn't stopped worrying about her alone on the dark, snowy highway. My inner child wouldn't stop holding its breath until she was at my side.

Our conversation woke Travis, who stood and hugged them too, then I introduced them to Kathy and McKay. Janice and Emily wanted to hear everything. They cried with me as I filled them in on Elora. I asked Emily about Hudson, and how his treatments were going. Emily was telling her own difficult story when Travis peered over my head at the clock on the wall. "What time is it?"

I shrugged. I hadn't noticed.

"Elora's been gone well over an hour." He searched for the shoes he'd kicked off. "I think I'll go find out what's going on."

"Okay, but come right back," I said, and didn't let go of his arm until he'd bent low so I could kiss his cheek.

Kathy asked Emily and Janice more about their families. Twenty minutes passed.

What's taking so long? Why isn't he back?

Maybe the doctor had been hard to find. Maybe the MRI was taking longer than expected and Travis was still waiting for news. Maybe Travis had stopped to get a snack or use the restroom. There were plenty of logical explanations.

No need to panic.

Minutes continued to creep by while Emily filled me in on what I should expect from chemo and radiation. I kept sneaking glances at the clock. Twenty-five minutes. Thirty.

Where is he?

The door opened. I exhaled, relieved that Travis had finally returned, but instead, a young woman I didn't recognize entered. Her hair was dark and fell with a natural curl just beneath her chin, her bangs held back in a simple metal clip.

"Mrs. Isaacson? Is there a Mrs. Isaacson?"

"That's me." I stood, passing Noah to Janice.

"Would it be all right if we spoke outside?"

"Of course," I said, following the young woman into the hallway as adrenaline shot lightning through my veins.

She stopped just outside the door and faced me, speaking very fast.

"My name is Jennifer. I'm a social worker here at the hospital. Things are not going well with your daughter, and your husband sent me to find you."

Her words sliced me open, but there was no time to bleed. Elora was in trouble. I had to go to her. Now.

"Where is she?"

"Her heart has stopped, and she's being resuscitated. Do you want me to take you to her?"

"Yes!" I said forcefully. "Take me!"

"Are you sure? It will be very hard for you to see."

"Yes! I'm sure!"

"Okay. This way."

Jennifer grabbed my forearm and hurried me into a fast walk.

"I'll fill you in."

She explained that as the doctors prepared Elora for her MRI, the fluid and pressure in her head rose to critical levels again. She went into cardiac arrest. They resuscitated her once and tried to get the MRI, but her heart stopped again. They resuscitated her a second time, but were unable to do the scan before her heart stopped for a third time.

"They're doing CPR on her right now. But it isn't going well," Jennifer said.

Wild emotions boiled in my chest, threatening to erupt, but I forced them down deep. Elora needed me, and I wouldn't be able to help her if I lost it now. I thrust my heart into a steely cage as Jennifer and I quickened our pace down the hall.

"Where is she now?" I asked, almost running.

"They're preparing her for a CT scan to get as much info as

possible about her tumor. Emergency surgery might be her only hope."

"And Travis is with her?"

"Yes."

"How close are we?" I would not let anything more happen to her without me there.

"It's just ahead." But then, Jennifer unexpectedly grabbed my arm, forcing me to stop. I turned to her, bewildered.

"How are you doing this?" Jennifer the professional was gone, and in her place stood a young woman with tears in her eyes.

"What?" I didn't know what she was asking.

"How are you not a puddle on the floor?"

"I..."

I didn't have an answer. There wasn't time to think. I just felt...strengthened. God had shown me that He and Christ were with me. And I had Travis, and the family in the waiting room, and more on the way.

And...others. Suddenly I just knew. There were others. All around me, though I could not see them. I could feel them.

Aunt Patrice who had died when I was a little girl, and Grandpa Walker who passed away when I was pregnant with Elora. They were there, in that hallway, standing beside me, along with others.

Family for generations who knew me and loved me.

Just as my earthly loved ones had responded to my time of greatest need, so had my heavenly ones.

Looking into Jennifer's eyes, I gave the only explanation I had time for. "Because we are not alone here."

"Really?"

"Really."

Maybe she could feel it too, or maybe she just believed me. Either way, she nodded her head, resumed her social worker demeanor, and together we faced down the hallway and ran.

. . . All flesh is in mine hands;
be still and know that I am God.

DOCTRINE AND COVENANTS 101:16

13

GRAVITY

Jennifer pushed hard against a wooden door, flinging it open with the weight of her body. She turned quickly and pushed me by the shoulder into a nightmare.

Hot, stuffy air and a crush of bodies. Too many voices talking at once. Fifteen, maybe twenty nurses swarmed the room, running, grabbing, reaching, issuing orders, calling out vital signs.

I spotted Travis in the middle of the chaos, standing close to the bed, silent and pale.

A nurse moved to one side and I caught sight of Elora, stripped of all clothing, someone's large gloved hands pressing down on her frail chest. Pumping. Forcing her body hard into the bed over and over. A manual pump pressed over her nose and mouth squeezing breath into her lungs.

You're hurting her! I screamed in my mind, simultaneously accepting there was no other choice.

"Let's move!" someone shouted.

Travis backed away from the bed so the nurses could steer. I was frozen in place, unaware that I was standing in front of the door until Jennifer wrapped her arm around me and hauled me out of the way. The bed and mass of nurses flew past me into the hall.

"Where are they going?" I asked Jennifer.

"To the CT room."

Travis grabbed my hand, and we broke into a run behind the crowd.

This is a dream, a movie. Not real. Not Elora.

The nurse doing chest compressions tired, and another immediately took his place.

Seconds later, everyone rushed into a room that tasted of metal and rubber. A whirring came from the giant square-shaped machine that filled half the floor. Dr. Brockmeyer and three more doctors in white coats stood behind a glass wall, staring at a computer screen.

Jennifer instructed us to stand against the wall by the door. Travis wrapped his arms around my waist from behind and pressed my back against his chest. Jennifer stood next to us, acting as an interpreter, explaining everything.

A third nurse took over Elora's chest compressions. Others rushed to attach Elora's most vital monitors. Suddenly a flat, high-pitched scream filled the room—a heart monitor registering no beat, a flat yellow line scrolling across the screen. I could not tear my eyes away.

"Breathe, baby, breathe," I begged Elora under the noise of voices and machines. I squeezed the words into the air, pushing them across the room, willing them into her mind. I needed her to hear me. "Please, baby. Breathe."

It took all of my willpower not to run to Elora, push all of those people away from her, and make her listen to me. Make her breathe.

"Do you still want to stay?" Jennifer asked.

"Yes," Travis and I answered together.

Travis pressed his lips against my ear. "Pray."

I started to shake. My hands. My arms. My shoulders and chest. My own breathing, faster and faster, as the monitor continued to scream.

Father, please! I shouted in my mind and imagined a round conduit above my head opening straight into heaven. One prayer would not be enough. I would plead with God nonstop until Elora was safe. *Please!*

I continued my silent prayer, at the same time calling out loud to Elora. "Come on, baby girl, come on! Come back!" *Please God, let her take a breath!* "Please, baby, you can do it. Mommy's right here!"

Travis joined in, calling out his own encouragement. "Breathe, Elora. Breathe for Daddy, please!"

Jennifer asked again, "Do you still want to stay?"

"Yes." I would not abandon my child, not now, no matter how painful it was to witness. "Pleeease!" The word tore painfully from my throat, reaching to God, the nurses, Elora, anyone who would hear.

And then a sound.

Beep . . . Beep . . . Beep.

Weak, and far apart, but still there.

"That's a heartbeat." I grabbed Jennifer by the hand. "That's a heartbeat, right?"

Jennifer confirmed that it was.

Oh, thank you, Father! I called heavenward.

But the nurse continued to do chest compressions on Elora. Jennifer explained that if they stopped, they might lose the heartbeat. And they could only do the scan if Elora's heart kept beating.

A nurse knocked on the glass wall and gave Dr. Brockmeyer a thumbs-up. He immediately ran into the room. "Vests!" he shouted, and everyone grabbed heavy lead-lined aprons from hooks on the walls.

Jennifer grabbed the last two vests and handed one to Travis and one to me. There wasn't one left for her. Travis insisted she take his. She started to protest, but Travis said, "You're here to take care of our girl, and you *will* take this from me."

She relented and put it on.

I told Travis to stay close behind me. My vest could shield us both.

A nurse climbed onto the bed and straddled Elora's legs, taking over the chest compressions that would keep her alive during the scan. Dr. Brockmeyer wheeled her bed under an arch in the center of the machine. Travis and I side-stepped along the wall to our left until we could see the top of Elora's head slide beneath the arch and back out. The emergency scan had only taken seconds.

Despite the continuous chest compressions, the heart monitor began its flat squeal again.

The nurses redoubled their CPR efforts.

Dr. Brockmeyer ran back into the computer room, briefly studied the screen, consulted with the other doctors, then waved for us to hurry and join them.

Jennifer took the lead vest from my hands. Travis and I hurried around the back of the CT machine, stepping over rows of thick black cables and plugs so we wouldn't interfere with the nurses still trying to save Elora.

Once in the glass-walled room, Dr. Brockmeyer rushed ahead. "I don't have time to explain everything because if we don't act immediately, Elora will die."

I breathed heavily against the panic.

He gestured at the computer screen. Images from the CT scan glowed in green pixels.

"We need to do surgery, relieve her brain of as much pressure as we can, and hopefully remove the tumor. I wish we'd been able to do an MRI, but the best we can do is take what we see on the CT and guess."

Travis and I nodded.

"I think it's best if we go in here." He pointed to a spot on the left side of Elora's skull nearest the dark tumor mass. "It's risky at best, but my associates agree that if we do nothing, she *will* die."

Travis and I looked at the three white-coated doctors. All three men confidently nodded their agreement. It was all we needed.

Together, Travis and I said, "Go!"

Dr. Brockmeyer did not need to be told twice. He ran into the CT room calling orders while Travis and I scribbled our signatures onto surgical consent forms. With practiced cooperation, the medical team prepped Elora to move in seconds. A nurse climbed back onto Elora's bed to continue chest compressions so the bed could be pushed faster. Travis and I again found ourselves running with Jennifer down the hallway behind Elora and her team of lifesavers.

They put her into a large elevator, but there wasn't room for us.

Jennifer quickly assessed the situation. "If you want one last chance to see your daughter, we need to take the stairs." She started to run back down the hallway. "This way. Hurry."

We made it to the top of the stairs with only seconds to spare before the team raced out of the elevator, past us into the operating room.

But it was enough time for a final precious glance. A flash of auburn hair. An eye, mostly closed. Air pump pressed over her nose and mouth. Gloved hands on her pale chest, pressing. Pressing.

A microscopic glance, and then...

She was gone.

Through doors where I could not follow.

Not knowing if I would ever see her alive again.

I stood helplessly in the corridor, imploring God to go with her. I knew He would, but my own uselessness cut bitterly. Heavy, stinging, messy tears blurred my vision and dripped from my chin. I turned to face Travis and Jennifer, raised my hands in front of me and let them fall to my side, defeated. Jennifer didn't say a word. She just put her arm around my shoulder and let me cry. Travis crouched with his back against a wall, hands over his face, but I guessed he was crying too.

When, after several minutes, my heaving sobs slowed, Jennifer led us back to the elevator and down to a small consultation room just outside the PICU doors.

"If the doctors and nurses have any news, they'll know to find you here," she said.

The room was tiny, with no windows, only four blue cloth-covered chairs and a simple oak end table topped with a tatty silk flower arrangement and a box of tissues. The white-faced clock on the wall ticked audibly in the silence. I sat on one of the chairs.

"Do you want anything? Something to eat or drink?" Jennifer asked.

Neither of us did.

She promised to keep us posted, then left us alone.

Travis sat down beside me and held my hand, words that needed to be said hanging heavily between us. A raw, burning realization in both our hearts that our Elora might not make it. Words I couldn't bear to voice for fear they meant I was giving up on my child. Giving up on God and any chance of a miracle.

I released Travis's hand, preferring to pace circles around the claustrophobic room as heavy, aching sobs poured from a fear I had never known. I didn't want to talk or be comforted. I just wanted to cry for as long and hard as it took for the pain to siphon out of my soul. My cheeks and nose grew raw from wiping at them with tissues.

I watched the clock obsessively. Every minute that passed, every minute no one came through the door meant there was hope she was still alive.

Travis and I alternated opening the door, looking down the hallway for any sign that someone was bringing us word. Forty-five minutes passed, and I wondered if I would go mad from the constant ticking of the clock.

Then there was a new sound—several hands knocking softly down low on the door. Travis swung it open and there stood three of the sweetest little faces in the world. I dropped to my knees and scooped Caleb, Shaustia, and Walker into a hug, smothering their precious cheeks with kisses. Travis's brother Jared stood with a nurse in the hallway. I looked at him through the doorway and mouthed, "Thank you." His timing couldn't have been more perfect. Jared smiled back at me and wiped his eyes, and the nurse said she would take him to the waiting room.

Travis scooted the four blue chairs into a circle and we all huddled close, warm in the comfort of togetherness. The kids were curious about what was happening.

"Elora is really sick," Travis told them.

"Is she going to be okay?" Shaustia asked.

"We don't know," I answered honestly.

"Is she going to die?" Caleb asked.

"Maybe," I answered, "but I hope not."

Caleb's face turned gray as I confirmed a fear he'd been carrying in his big-brother heart.

"Can we go and see her? Can we hug her?" Shaustia remained cheerfully optimistic.

"Not yet. She's still in surgery, but hopefully soon," Travis said, winking at me. I hoped it would be true too.

Walker was too young to understand what was happening. He mostly sat on my lap, tracing the red places on my eyes and cheeks with one gentle little finger.

There was another knock on the door, and I froze. I didn't want the children to be in the room if we were about to receive bad news. Travis opened the door and a nurse said, "Your mother is here."

I burst into the hall. Mom stood just a few steps away. I ran to her. She wrapped her arms around me, and we cried all the tears we'd been holding back until we could cry them together. Her voice, her scent, her touch flowed over my ache like a balm. I soaked her in until I had cried myself out. I lifted my face from her shoulder, leaving sticky wet spots all over her jacket.

I fished a used tissue from my pocket. "Mom, I'm so glad you're here."

"I'm so glad I'm here too. Heavenly Father helped me the whole way. He kept me awake, and I never stopped praying that I'd get here in time. *Am* I in time?" She started to cry again, fearful of my answer.

"I hope so, Mom. She's in surgery. I don't know if she's alive. But no matter what, I need you here so much." My voice broke and I couldn't talk anymore, so I hugged her again, thankful beyond words that God had delivered her safely to me.

After a long hug, she pushed me back so she could look into my eyes.

"Sweetheart, when was the last time you and Travis were in the waiting room?"

"Not for a while. But Noah's there with Janice. I haven't fed him for I don't know how long. Could you check on him?"

"I already did. He's completely fine." Mom had borrowed a bottle and some formula from Jared and Jenn, and hungry Noah had gulped it down without a fuss. "When you're ready, you and Travis should check in. The whole room is filled with people who all seem to know each other, and I have a feeling they're here for you."

"How many, Mom? Who?"

"So many I didn't count, but there's no more room to sit, and hardly a spot left to stand."

I pictured the big, dark waiting room.

Full?

Mom listed a few of the people she recognized. "And I know there are many more on their way."

It was as if Elora's illness had created a spot of gravity, and the people Travis and I loved were being drawn toward it. An army of support.

I didn't want to leave the small consultation room until I had word of Elora, but knowing I had angels surrounding me and a waiting room full of friends and family just down the hall shored up my courage. Whatever news the surgeon was about to bring, they had all come to help me bear it.

14

HOLDING ON

MOM OFFERED to take Caleb, Shaustia, and Walker to the waiting room to see the fish tank. I almost didn't let them go. A powerful protective yearning surged through my body, urging me to hold them close, shield them, never let them out of my sight. Never let anything bad happen to them. But keeping them with me meant they would have to sit in that tiny consultation room with nothing to entertain them, listening to their parents cry. And I definitely didn't want them in the room when the surgeon returned. I would be protecting them more if I let them go.

"You guys be good for Grandma, okay? We're right here if you need us."

Travis put an arm around my shoulder and leaned his cheek on the top of my head. Together, we watched Mom and the kids walk away, clinging to each other in a big grandma hug.

"You know. . ." he began.

"Know what?"

"Between your mom and mine, those kids are going to be quite spoiled today."

I smiled. "Yeah, but today they deserve it."

Alone now, we returned to the tiny consultation room. Travis and I paced and prayed for another excruciating hour and a half.

Finally, a knock on the door. Jennifer the social worker stepped into the room and I leaped in front of her, frantic for news.

"Why don't we all sit down," she said.

People only ask you to sit down when they have something bad to tell you.

But I found myself sitting anyway on the edge of the chair's worn blue upholstery, a tissue held to my painfully raw nose, tears already falling in anticipation of the news I feared most.

Jennifer clasped her hands together. "I can't believe I get to tell you this, but Elora survived her surgery, and she's on her way back to you right now."

I sat up straight. "Wait...for real? She's alive?"

Travis whipped his head around to me, shocked. "I didn't think there was any way."

"Me neither!"

"Now, please understand," Jennifer cautioned, "things are still very critical, and Elora's prognosis is not good. Dr. Brockmeyer will be here in a few minutes to tell you more, but I wanted you to at least know she's alive."

I leaned forward and hugged her. "Thank you. We've been in agony not knowing."

"You're welcome. I'm happy you get more time with her." Jennifer left to find the doctor and bring him to us.

When the door closed, Travis and I allowed ourselves a quiet cheer. Elora was alive. It didn't matter if it was for an hour or a hundred years—time had become the most precious commodity of our world. Any amount was a miracle.

Less than ten minutes later, Jennifer led Dr. Brockmeyer into the room.

"Hi, Travis and Krista," he said, weariness peeking around the sides of his broad smile. He sat in the chair next to Jennifer, across from me and Travis.

"I'd like to tell you about Elora's operation, what we found, and how she's doing now."

I snatched a fresh tissue from the box, just in case.

"As you know, Elora went into surgery under active CPR, but we were able to stabilize her enough to begin the surgery. We shaved the left side of her head and made a large C-shaped incision. I removed a portion of her skull, located the tumor, and extracted a large piece of it, which I sent to pathology for evaluation. But it looks like a small round blue cell tumor, which we mostly find in children."

"Is it cancer?" Travis asked.

Cancer or not, please tell me it's treatable.

"We won't know for sure until pathology sends back the results."

Travis and I nodded again.

"Now for the hard stuff." The doctor paused to gather his thoughts. "Elora's body has gone through some pretty significant trauma, and things aren't looking good."

But there's a way to fix it, right?

Dr. Brockmeyer spoke slowly so Travis and I would be able to internalize every word. "I'd hoped to remove the entire tumor, but Elora's heart stopped a few more times during surgery. We were able to bring her back every time she coded, but her heart has sustained a lot of damage and she was too unstable to continue the operation. I closed up her head, but left off the section of skull to allow room for her brain to swell."

"So... she has no bone on one side of her head?" I repeated, ill from the realization of how much trauma Elora had experienced.

"Yes. That's right." The doctor paused, but a sharp intake of breath hinted there was more he needed to say.

"But the tumor isn't our biggest problem anymore. The CT scan showed evidence of multiple strokes, and the intense pressure on her brain has caused internal bleeding which we've had trouble controlling. She received several blood transfusions during the operation. Her brain has sustained even further damage due to repeated lack of oxygen. And on top of her heart damage, several of her ribs are broken, and her lungs are filled with fluid from the chest compressions."

I couldn't stop from imagining it all happening to my girl in horrific detail. I twisted my head back and forth, trying to shake loose the images.

Elora's broken. And he's trying to tell me he can't fix her.

No! I snapped back at the voice in my head.

But it did no good because Dr. Brockmeyer blew his breath out slowly and finished what he had really come to say. "All in all, it's amazing she's still alive. And the machines keeping her alive will give you time to be with her and decide what you want to do. But guys, understand. The amount of damage in her body is *very* extensive, and there is little chance she can survive."

"But what if there's a miracle and she does?" Travis blurted out.

"Yes, you're right, I've seen miracles that I can't explain. And I don't want to dissuade you from that, but Elora's brain is so damaged that even if she does survive, she'll be in an extreme vegetative state for the rest of her life."

From the moment I became a mother, my worst nightmares involved something horrible happening to one of my children.

And now it was happening. With those words, the doctor had just turned the nightmare real. Whether she lived or died, my Elora was never coming back.

My mind filled with all the golden hopes I'd ever wished for Elora's life—her first day of kindergarten, her baptism, first date, high school prom, graduation, wedding day. One by one, they shriveled and turned to ash.

I couldn't bear it, staring down the path of my future, constrained to one of two destinations, both horrific—an entire life without my daughter, or an entire life caring for my severely handicapped daughter. Shame colored my cheeks as I silently admitted to myself that I didn't know which I feared more. Either way, I had lost her.

Dr. Brockmeyer asked if we had any other questions, but I was too numb to think of any. "Then I'll head back to Elora." He stood slowly on exhausted legs. "When we move her into the PICU and get her settled, I'll have a nurse come find you in the waiting room."

"Dr. Brockmeyer?" I said as he turned to leave.

"Yes?" he answered.

"Thank you for doing everything you could for Elora. Even if it doesn't save her life, you made it so we can see her again."

He sniffed hard and blinked unexpected tears from his tired eyes, then waved his hand behind him as he and Jennifer walked out the door.

Misery pressed on my heart like a flooded river about to overflow its banks.

"Trav?" I started to cry.

"I know." Travis reached for me.

I buried my face in his shoulder and cried from a depth of

pain I didn't know existed. Wailing, primal sobs tore through my body. Travis squeezed me tightly and cried tears onto my scalp. I grasped his shirt with both hands, frightened by the uncontrollable anguish surging around me.

"What . . . are we going . . . to do?" I choked out.

Travis couldn't talk. He just shook his head.

I'd been clinging to the hope of Elora's full recovery like a life preserver. With it yanked from my grasp, I sank into blackness, torrents of despair lapping at my chin. With every wail of grief for Elora, the current dragged me further under.

She'll never open her eyes again. Never smile. Never say my name, or suck her fingers, or put her arms around my neck…

The anguish was too swift, too strong.

I dove into my hazy memories of the hour before Elora's first seizure, frantic to recall the little things I'd never guessed would be her last.

When did I last see her awake? What were the last words she said? Last smile?

The details had been swept away in the muddy, churning rapids of Elora's sudden decline. I hadn't known to pay attention. Hadn't guessed the importance of soaking in every word, every flutter of her eyelashes, every touch.

I couldn't remember. And I'd never get another chance.

All the millions of tiny things that made up Elora's personality were locked away forever in her broken body.

I let go of Travis and sank into a chair, agony leeching the strength from my body.

I could not breathe, could not calm my fear, could not save myself.

I was drowning.

Like Peter.

An image came to mind of the New Testament apostle who had walked on water for a short time until fear overpowered his faith and he began to sink.

Panicked, he cried out, "Lord, save me."

"And immediately Jesus stretched forth his hand, and caught him" (Matthew 14:30-31).

Just like Peter, my fear was overpowering. And just like Peter, I needed Jesus to hold me above the waves.

I reached my hand high above my head and cried out in my mind, "Save me!" I envisioned Christ's hand reaching down, wrapping His fingers firmly around my wrist as I grasped on to His. The fierce waters continued to rage around me, but I had made my choice. I would hold on to Jesus, trusting that He would never let me go. That He would keep my head above water. That He would not let me drown.

When thou passest through the waters,
I will be with thee; and through the rivers,
they shall not overflow thee: when thou walkest
through the fire, thou shalt not be burned.

ISAIAH 43:2

15

MOTHER'S INTUITION

THE WAITING ROOM beckoned. Our friends and family had waited hours for news about Elora, and now that we had it, we owed it to them. And Travis and I were anxious to receive the love and support that awaited us there.

We abandoned the tiny consultation room. While we walked, I tried to clean myself up a bit, dabbing at the salty tracks on my face with the sleeve of my sweatshirt, but the well-worn fleece stung my cheeks and nose. Like fine sandpaper, hundreds of tissues had wiped away layers of my skin.

Outside the waiting room, the murmur of familiar voices floated through the wooden door. My resolve disintegrated. How could I face them? There would be hope for Elora shining in their eyes. They didn't know the news we were bringing. They hadn't heard the doctor talk about how broken Elora was. Somehow, Travis and I would have to tell them, then watch as their hope turned to sadness.

Why couldn't someone else do it? Anyone else?

Because they deserve to hear it from me.

I latched on to the anchor of Travis's hand. "We can do this,"

I said out loud as much to myself as to him. "We can. We can." And before either of us could change our minds, I turned the door handle and walked into the room.

All voices fell instantly silent as countless eyes turned in our direction. Every corner of the room was filled, just like Mom had said. Grandparents, parents, siblings. Aunts, uncles, cousins. Nieces, nephews. Neighbors and friends, old and new. More than I'd imagined. Some I hadn't expected. All so beautiful and precious, each face radiating pristine love.

"Mama! Daddy!" Caleb, Shaustia, and Walker ran to us, hugging our waists and legs. I lifted Walker and kissed his cheeks. They were sticky. "Bof grandmas gave us treats!" he announced, then all three kids ran back to a mess of coloring books and games scattered on the floor. Baby Noah sat happily gurgling on Uncle Jared's lap.

My mom ushered us farther into the room. "Everyone is anxious for news. If you stand here, they should all be able to hear you."

People turned in their seats or stood up from the floor and moved closer. When they were resettled, Travis began, "Uh, wow, everyone, this is amazing. We didn't expect so many of you." His voice broke, and he paused to compose himself. "Krista and I are more thankful for your support than we can say."

I chimed in, tears barely restrained. "Yes, everyone, thank you. This is so much easier not being alone."

Travis looked at me, and I nodded that he should proceed.

"We just met with Elora's neurosurgeon, and first of all, we want to tell you she made it through surgery . . ." A collective sigh blew through the room, then chattering as people commented about their relief. Travis raised his voice over the chatter to continue, " . . . but there's also some hard news."

Travis reiterated the doctor's description of all that was wrong with Elora. I held on to his arm with both hands and observed the room—face after face strained with worry, horrified by the list of Elora's injuries, hands over open mouths, heads shaking in disbelief. I would have given anything to trade places with anyone in the room, to be the one sitting out there instead of the one standing up front in despair. But if it really came down to it, who would I choose? Which of their children would I pick to take Elora's place? Which parent would I condemn to the pain and darkness of watching their child suffer?

Not one of them.

Travis finished his report, but there was still one question on everyone's mind. McKay called out, "What did the doctor say about recovery? What are her chances?"

I shook my head and whispered, "Not good. Not good." It was the pebble that smashed the dam. I covered my face in front of them all and cried. Then there were arms, so many of them, passing me around the room, crying with me, holding me tight, holding me together.

After I'd hugged them all, Mom led me to a rocking chair surrounded by extended family. Travis stood on the other side of the fish tank being comforted by friends from our neighborhood. Granny Hansen handed me a fresh tissue. Conversations picked up again, everyone talking about Elora.

Uncle Porter brought me a plastic container filled with a hamburger and fries. I smiled my gratitude at him. The food was warm and fresh. I wanted to be hungry, but the usually tempting aroma of grilled meat and fried food only made me sick.

Mom knelt on the floor by my knee. "Honey, try to eat. You need your strength."

I obeyed and took a bite, chewed and chewed and swallowed. I tried a French fry and then another. My mouth was dry, and nothing tasted the way it should. It was exhausting. "Mom, will you see if Travis wants some of this? It's more than I can eat."

She moved in closer to whisper, "Porter already offered to get him his own, but he says he's fasting." Travis had been going without food and water since our meager meal in the cafeteria as a sign to God of our faith and a petition for a miracle.

As a nursing mother, fasting was unhealthy for both me and my baby. Travis had kept his fast quiet so I wouldn't feel bad eating and drinking in front of him. I stared at my husband across the room, in awe of his selflessness.

After I'd done my best with the hamburger, Jared brought Noah to me. Rocking softly, I tried to nurse him, but trauma and exhaustion had dried up more than just my hope and I settled for feeding him a bottle, amazed at how well he gulped down the formula. He snuggled to sleep on my chest. I closed my eyes and leaned my head back into the padded chair, enveloped by voices from my whole life. I allowed myself the child-like comfort of being cradled by my loved ones. Their voices blended to a soothing hum, lulling me toward sleep until an unfamiliar voice sounded above the others.

"Mr. and Mrs. Isaacson?"

A nurse had come to fetch us. It was time to see Elora.

Travis, Mom, and I followed the nurse to the PICU doors, where she took a phone receiver from the wall and announced us. A buzzer granted admission and the doors swung open.

The long, far wall of the PICU was divided into cubicles

hung with blue curtains on sliding metal rings. Several open curtains revealed tiny patients wearing oxygen masks, signs at the ends of their beds warning of respiratory infection.

The nurse caught me looking. "That's why we recommend you don't bring your baby in here. It could be very dangerous for him."

"What about my other kids?"

"We'll allow Elora's older siblings to come in, but no other children under the age of twelve."

Mom put her hand on my shoulder. "Don't worry about the baby or the kids. I'll make sure they're all taken care of."

The nurse retrieved two blue hospital wristbands from behind the counter with Elora's name printed above a barcode. She attached one to my wrist and the other to Travis's, tagging us as Elora's parents.

"Dr. Moon?" The nurse spoke to a trim middle-aged woman in a white lab coat, her wavy light-brown hair pulled into a loose low ponytail. She looked up from the medical chart in her hands as the nurse said, "These are the Isaacsons."

The doctor walked around the counter toward us, hand extended.

"Hello. I'm Dr. Moon, head of the Pediatric Intensive Care Unit."

Travis, Mom, and I introduced ourselves. Dr. Moon reopened the medical file, flipping pages. "I've just been catching up on Elora's records." Her eyes scanned the reports. "Dr. Brockmeyer filled you in on her surgery?"

"Yes, he did," Travis confirmed.

"You've all been through a lot today and I'm sure you're anxious to see your daughter, so I won't delay." Dr. Moon showed us to a door directly behind the nurses' station.

"This is the room for our most critical patients. There's always someone just a step away." I relaxed a little. If Elora needed help, it was right outside her door.

"Just a couple things before you go in. Remember to be careful around Elora's incision site. That's where she's missing the piece of skull bone. It's a very vulnerable spot, so be cautious. And we haven't had time to clean her up very much, but I guessed you wouldn't want to wait."

"Good guess," I agreed. She gave me a small understanding smile.

Dr. Moon opened the door...and there was my girl.

I rushed to her side, planting kisses over every inch of exposed skin.

Elora's face was pale, translucent, speckled here and there with tiny red droplets that hinted at the battle she'd fought. Her head was completely shaved but for a small patch of hair over her right ear, a hopelessly snarled bird's nest matted with dried blood. The huge C-shaped incision, tinged orange with antiseptic, covered the left side of her head, the skin held together with too many biting metal staples. She wore a clean pair of child's pajamas, her chest, arms, legs, head, and face attached to a spider web of tubes, wires, drains, and monitors. The whole room whirred and beeped.

Elora would most likely never open her eyes again or say my name, but for now, her hands were warm, her cheeks were velvet, and her little chest rose and fell in cadence with the machines in the room. Her fingers and toes still had bits of nail polish on them, and when I kissed her left hand, those two middle sucking fingers mercifully retained the last remnant of her baby scent while the rest of her body had succumbed to aromas of antiseptic and bleached sheets.

I held her fingers to my nose and breathed, conflicted between despair at the evident trauma Elora had endured and elation that she had survived.

I moved aside and allowed my mother to take my place, to finally say hello to the grandchild she had driven four hundred miles through snowy darkness to see. She held Elora's hand, whispering secrets I could not hear, and cried.

Travis rubbed Elora's feet, tears falling freely.

Dr. Moon stood silently in front of the door. Travis asked her, "What now? What do we do?"

She answered, "We watch and wait to see if anything changes, but right now, you spend time with her."

"Is that all? Is there anything that hasn't been tried?" Travis pleaded to know.

Dr. Moon had probably been asked those same questions by hundreds of parents. With experienced compassion, she explained, "I know you wish there were clear answers, but Elora has suffered significantly. As Dr. Brockmeyer explained, there's very little chance that she will survive. But for now, you have *time.*"

She stressed the last word, holding my gaze like she was trying to find a path around what doctors are supposed to say and what she wished she could tell me.

We have time.

Perhaps time was all we had left. And if that's what Dr. Moon was hinting at, I was done wasting any more of it.

I took my place in a chair at Elora's side. For the rest of the day, all I wanted was to be her mother. I leaned across the bed as close to Elora as possible, and for the first time since her first seizure, I stopped counting out agonizing seconds like an obsessed metronome. I caressed her skin and sang her favorite lullaby, low and sweet, while time spooled around us like an unmarked length of satin ribbon.

Travis and I held constant vigil at the bedside through the afternoon, elbows leaning on the mattress even after they were rubbed raw. Mom escorted visitors in and out of the room in hospital-approved groups of two or three. Some interacted with Elora. Others felt content to stand back and observe. But each of them blessed the room with their love and faith, transforming an ordinary space into a sanctuary, a bubble of reverence, introspection, and love. Even the seasoned nurses working quietly around us sensed the change, often excusing themselves to wipe tears and steady their emotions.

The light through the windows in the PICU turned golden, then orange, and still Travis and I kept our vigil while the visitors continued to file in. Between groups, Dr. Moon stepped in to speak with us.

"You know how I keep reminding you that you have time?" Travis and I nodded. "Well, Elora's time is becoming very precious, and you still have a very large group in the waiting room. I'm going to suspend the small group rule for now and open the doors. Bring in as many people as you need to."

Travis perked up and said to me, "Let's have a family prayer."

Fifty or sixty family members streamed through the PICU doors into Elora's room, crowding around her bed. Mom even covered Noah with a blanket in his car seat and rushed him safely into the room.

Our social worker, Jennifer, offered to meet with us and our three older children to prepare them to see Elora. We brought Caleb, Shaustia, and Walker back to the small consultation room.

Jennifer explained, "Every person mourns differently. It's important to let everyone mourn however they need to. That means we don't force anyone to do anything they aren't comfortable with." She knelt down to speak on the same level as the children. "When you see your sister, she's going to look a little different than she did before. But she's still the same sister. You can talk to her and touch her if you want, but it's also okay if you *don't* want to."

Jennifer stood again. "Mom and Dad, just be there for them. They'll show you what they need."

It proved to be just the counsel we needed. As we entered Elora's room, the crowd quieted and moved aside to make room for our family to approach the bed. Walker asked dozens of questions about the noisy machines and wanted to sit on the bed so he could kiss Elora's hand. Shaustia wondered how soon Elora would come home, then shared dozens of funny memories about her sister and showed everyone that she and Elora wore the same color of fingernail polish. But Caleb immediately hid in a corner of the room and wouldn't talk.

Caleb had always been closest to Elora. At their young ages of nine and two, they had a uniquely deep bond. When Caleb was four years old, he'd been diagnosed with obsessive-compulsive disorder (OCD) and struggled with bouts of depression, explosive anger, and crying fits that could last hours despite my best efforts to soothe him. But one day during a particularly difficult episode, tiny Elora crawled up into Caleb's lap, and for some reason, he let her. They rocked each other, Elora sucking on her fingers, until Caleb was at peace. He trusted her with his heart after that day, and always asked for her when things got rough.

So when Caleb saw Elora in her hospital bed, hurt and unresponsive, he'd retreated to the corner of the room because his heart was breaking. And once again, I didn't know how to soothe him.

Caleb remained out of sight while the family group sang songs of our shared belief that we are all children of God, and that families can be together forever. Then everyone bowed their heads while Travis offered a prayer of faith and a plea for peace to settle in each heart. Finally, one by one, they all took a moment to approach the bed and express their love for Elora, each wondering if it would be their final chance.

Opening the door was difficult. No one wanted to separate themselves from the radiant love flooding the room. But most of them had spent hours in the waiting room and they were hungry and exhausted, including my children.

Travis's Aunt Linda offered to take Caleb, Shaustia, and Walker home with her to play with cousins and have some dinner. Walker and Shaustia were overjoyed at the prospect, but Caleb shrugged his shoulders and didn't move from the corner.

Linda gathered the kids' winter coats. "Do you want to say goodbye to your sister before we leave?"

Shaustia kissed Elora on the cheek. "I love you, Elora. Come home soon." My heart tore.

Travis lifted Walker so he could see Elora. He kissed her hand again. "Wuv you."

I knelt beside Caleb in the corner and ran my fingers through his thick brown hair. "Honey? Aunt Linda is ready to take you home. Do you want to come see Elora?"

He shook his head. His face twisted in pent-up unresolved pain. There was no way I could let him leave the hospital, or Elora, like that.

"Do you at least want to tell her you love her before you go?"

He shook his head harder.

Someone whispered, "Maybe he's scared."

Another voice, "I think he doesn't want to leave his mom."

More and more opinions.

"Caleb, come on, buddy. You don't want to leave without saying goodbye."

"Krista, make him. He'll regret it forever if he doesn't."

"Caleb, Elora needs to know you love her."

I raised my hand to the crowd. The voices quieted. I drew Caleb's lanky arms toward me until he relented and moved into my lap. Intuition screamed that there was more to his silence. Something he was afraid to say. But there wasn't time to coax it from him like I would have at home.

Heavenly Father, I need you again. You've helped me every time I've asked, and now I have a son here who's hurting. And I need to help him right now. Father, will you help me know what's wrong?

Like ticker tape, a question typed itself across my mind. I leaned close to Caleb's ear and whispered the words to him. "Are you afraid to tell Elora goodbye because you think she'll die if you do?"

His arms flew to my neck, his face pressed into my shoulder. Explosive wailing. "She can't die! And I won't say goodbye because she can't leave until I say goodbye. So, I won't ever say it, and she won't ever die."

I rocked him like Elora would have and cried with him while he wailed long and loud.

Father in Heaven, I can't let him leave like this.

Another idea.

"Caleb? You know how Elora is the one who helps you when you're having a hard time?"

He nodded his head and cried harder.

"Heavenly Father wants you to know He understands that. But if Elora does die, did you know she can still be with you?"

He didn't stop crying, but raised his head from my shoulder.

"If she goes to heaven, you'll have an angel who loves you so much, and who can come to you whenever you need her."

"But I still don't want her to die." His face was smeared and red and desperate.

"Oh, sweetie, I don't want that either."

We rocked and swayed in time to the whirring machines and cried together until he'd let out all the things he'd been holding back. And outside, the descending sun pricked itself on the edge of the earth and bled crimson over the horizon.

16

TIME

CALEB EVENTUALLY SOOTHED. Linda, Shaustia, and Walker waited patiently by the door as he wiped his cheeks with the heels of his hands and approached Elora's bed.

He didn't touch her. He only said, "Luz you," mimicking Elora's two-year-old way of saying, "I love you."

An unexpected pin pricked my heart.

Elora will never say that again.

Caleb looked at me, unsure how to end the one-sided conversation with his sister. I wrapped my arm around his shoulder.

"She loves you too, honey. I know she heard you."

Though he didn't smile, the interaction seemed enough to stave off his anguish. He let Linda help him into his coat.

Travis and I kissed the kids' faces as they left, relieved they were headed somewhere comfortable and safe, where they'd remain mercifully unaware.

Slowly, family members finished their goodbyes to Elora and trickled from the room. Mom took baby Noah back to the waiting room, and I resumed my place at Elora's side. Travis sat in a chair on the opposite side of the bed. He reached across Elora's blanketed legs to hold my hand.

Late-afternoon visitors ebbed and flowed from Elora's room while nurses faithfully cared for her.

My arms grew weary leaning across the mattress, heavy with the ache of wanting to pull Elora closer. I hadn't held her since the nurse started her first IV nearly twenty-four hours earlier.

I whispered aloud, "I wish I could hold her."

A nurse quietly checking a monitor directly behind me overheard. "Didn't anyone tell you that you can?"

I sat straight up. "Really? I can? I can hold her *now*?"

"Yes." She smiled at my enthusiasm. "Let me finish up here, and I'll go get a couple more nurses to help. It takes a lot of hands to lift her and shift all of her equipment at the same time."

I glanced at the massive web of tubes and wires crisscrossing Elora's bed and body. "Yeah. I bet."

"Oh, and you might want to use the restroom while you can. Once we get her onto your lap, you won't be going anywhere for a while."

I took the nurse's advice and returned in time to see Travis hoist a cushioned rocking chair into the room and place it beside Elora's bed. I sat.

It took the nurses several minutes to prepare Elora to be moved, sorting through the tubes and wires, unhooking some, securing the vital ones, clarifying who would move what. A blanket was placed over my lap, followed by a large blue pad connected to a pump submerged in a basin of ice water. Elora had developed a high fever, and the cooling mat would help lower her temperature.

When everything was set, one nurse slipped her hands under Elora's shoulders, then paused and said, "Before we move her, I need to inform you of the risk that the intubation tube could come loose or be pulled out completely. If that happens, we won't be able to re-intubate her. And if that happens, she won't live. Do you understand and accept the risk?"

I had begun to suspect that the doctors and nurses did not expect Elora to live much longer. No one had said it in such plain terms, but there was something about the way her care had changed. The careful, attentive, but unhurried staff, the lack of any future plans or procedures, and the repeated reminder to every question Travis and I asked about Elora, "You have time."

I'd assumed Dr. Moon and the nurses were simply reminding us of the gift of spending time at Elora's side, but the more they said it, I began to guess at what they really meant. Time was a merciful kindness they were providing. Every minute they fought to keep Elora alive gave us time to come to terms with losing her at our own pace.

And if this gift of time was truly as brief as I feared, why would I not risk holding Elora in my arms one more time? The need in my heart grossly outweighed the risk.

But I wasn't the only one who needed to give approval. I looked at Travis. "You okay with this?"

He didn't hesitate. "Absolutely. She needs her mama."

I could no longer talk around the lump in my throat, so I gave the nurses a go-ahead nod.

"Lift on three. One, two, three." Two nurses lifted Elora's limp body while a third hefted handfuls of equipment. They placed Elora on my lap with her head over my right arm, her legs draped over my left. She was longer and heavier than I remembered, as if trauma had stretched her, weighted her body. But her weight lightened mine.

It took several minutes more for the nurses to reconnect and secure all the equipment. They wrapped tubes around my shoulders and pinned wires to my sweatshirt to keep them in place. One of the nurses propped pillows between my elbows and the rocking chair's wooden armrests. Slowly, the beeping and whirring returned to the room as the machines picked up where they'd left off.

Travis sat in a chair close to Elora's head. I pressed her to my body as tightly as I dared and closed my eyes. We rocked. And for a moment I was home and she was simply sleeping.

I held Elora for one hour, then two, rocking unceasingly as if the motion could draw out time, erase what had happened, stop the future from coming.

The past.

The future.

I had no interest in entertaining such prickly companions. Not while Elora lay snuggled so perfectly in my arms. Not while I could feel her heart beating. I banished past and future, focusing only on the present moment, chiseling every second with her into stone memory.

While I held Elora, Travis's dad, Jeff, and stepmom, Lula, came into the room. Travis stood, relieved to see them, hug them, and witness them spend a few precious minutes of grandparent time with Elora.

Close friends Jesse and Trish stayed quietly at the edge of the room for a long time, watching me hold Elora. I often saw them speaking with my mom, making phone calls, or texting and discovered they were busy arranging help for our family—meals, childcare, and other necessities—so Travis and I could feel free to stay in the hospital with Elora as long as we needed. Their foresight lifted concerns from my shoulders I hadn't realized were there.

I only had one request. That anyone who entered my home would leave Elora's things exactly as they were, every evidence of her personality untouched, left for me to discover when I returned.

Krista and Travis holding Elora on
January 19, 2007

Mom got a phone call and left the room. A few minutes later, she came back with a huge smile...and my dad. Aunt Janice had called him as soon as I rushed from the PICU waiting room with the social worker to be with Elora. With the help of family and friends, he miraculously secured a seat on the last flight that night out of Boise. Dad was the last family member Elora had been waiting for. And I'd been praying nonstop that he'd make it in time.

"Dad!" I would have run to him, but I was still holding Elora, both of us bound in tubes and wires. I couldn't move, so he came to me. My strong, quiet father, who always kept his feelings so well guarded, saw me holding my broken Elora and fell to his knees beside us.

"I'm so sorry, Krista." He barely got the words out. We cried together. He stroked Elora's cheek so gently with his rough carpenter's hand.

Mom prompted, "Tell her you're here, Dave"

"Elora, Grandpa's here." It was all he could say.

He didn't know it, but I needed to hear those words as much as Elora did.

Dr. Moon came in to check on us. "Hello, everyone. How's our girl?"

Dad quickly wiped his face before he stood and moved aside. Dr. Moon placed a hand on my shoulder and looked kindly down at Elora in my arms.

Travis said, "We're hoping *you* can tell us how she's doing."

"Well, that's actually why I'm here."

Mom and Dad took the cue that this was going to be a heavy conversation and led all of the visitors from the room.

Dr. Moon waited until the door closed before she continued. "I wish I was coming with better news, but Elora's vital signs aren't improving. In fact, all indications show that her organs are beginning to shut down. At this point, there's not much more we can do except make her as comfortable as possible."

I had been steeling myself for this conversation, internally rehearsing how it might go. But it hadn't made me any more prepared to hear it because as the doctor said those words out loud, they became truth. A harsh reality that burned. Tears came hard and fast. I squeezed Elora's body tightly.

Not yet. Please, little one. Stay.

"How long?" Travis asked.

"A few days, a week at the most."

Travis blew heavily into his steepled fingers, and I let my head fall back against my chair, tears running sideways into my ears.

Dr. Moon allowed us a silent minute. I pressed Elora even tighter, tracking each thump of her heart, horrified by the thought of witnessing it stop forever.

Dr. Moon proceeded gently. "There are some things that I'd like to discuss with you, but only if you're ready."

I wasn't ready for any of it, but no amount of time was going to change that, so I nodded. Travis did too.

Dr. Moon's voice softened as she asked, "Have you considered organ donation?"

Checking the organ donation box on the driver's license renewal form had always been a simple decision when considering my own life, but it was never one I'd dreamed of making on behalf of my child. And yet I imagined there were other mothers out there, sitting beside other hospital beds, holding their children's hands, praying for a miracle. What if Elora could be that miracle for them?

Travis said, "Krista, I think we should at least consider it."

"I agree."

Dr. Moon said, "I'll ask one of our organ donation reps to review Elora's case. I'll also bring in a do-not-resuscitate order for you to sign if you'd like. It means that if her heart stops or she stops breathing, we won't perform any further life-saving procedures."

I understood that the do-not-resuscitate order was meant as a kindness to relieve Elora's body from further trauma. And I would sign it, even though it signified a point of surrender from which there was no return, a personal admission that the fight was ending. Great swelling tears leaked from the corners of my eyes. I ached for a private place to hide where no one would witness the implosion of my heart.

"One more thing." Dr. Moon said, "We have a volunteer in the hospital today who makes plaster castings of our most special patients' hands and feet. She's offered to make a set for you, as a gift."

I didn't want a statue of my child's hand. I wanted my child.

But I also didn't want to say no to this end-of-life service. What if one day I couldn't remember the shape of Elora's toes? Or the exact spot of the sucking blisters on her fingers?

"Yes, I'd like that," I said, though my tears confessed it wasn't completely true.

Dr. Moon looked down tenderly at Elora and rubbed her toes. "The volunteer is just outside in the PICU. Is it okay if I send her in?"

"Yes," I said.

Dr. Moon patted my arm, and as she left, I released the end of hope's string and cried out in terrible pain as it floated out of reach.

Our gift of time had nearly run out, the future agonizingly certain.

Elora was going to die.

And even with all my family and friends and angels and God surrounding me, I still didn't know how on earth I would survive it.

17

NIGHTMARE

THE LANYARD hanging from the volunteer's neck said her name was Lisa. She'd come in barely a minute after Dr. Moon left, and I wasn't as ready as I'd thought. I attempted to summon a smile for her, but my emotional reserve was drained. I had nothing left to give.

Lisa set a duffle bag on the counter and snapped blue latex gloves over her hands. "Would either of you like to help with the molds?"

What I really wanted was more time. More space. To breathe and think and hold Elora and cry. Her hourglass had been flipped for the last time and the sand was running, running. I couldn't hold it back. Couldn't stop it. But this kind woman had come, right now, to provide a service for me. It was now or never. It was a task to focus on. A chance to make one more memory with Elora.

Her body was still draped over both my arms, but in my mind, I reached a hand heavenward, grasping again for Jesus' hand, begging Him for strength, to keep holding me up.

"I'll help," I said to Lisa.

Travis pressed the nurse call button and asked them to move Elora from my lap back into her bed. Once Elora was settled, with all of her tubes and wires in their proper order, Lisa poured impression powder into a small plastic bucket and added water until the mixture was the consistency of pink ketchup. I lifted Elora's sucking-fingers hand and plunged it wrist-deep into the goo. Five minutes later, the mold had set like Silly Putty. Lisa pulled Elora's arm firmly but carefully until her hand popped out of the rubbery mold. We repeated the process with her left foot.

With the molds finished, Lisa wet a towel and wiped away the residue left on Elora's skin. "I'll pour the plaster casts right away. They usually take about an hour to dry. You'll be surprised by the detail." She glanced at Elora's feet. "They'll even show the little remnants of polish on her nails."

"Thank you." My smile was forced, but Lisa squeezed my hand encouragingly and smiled sweetly enough for the both of us. She packed away her supplies and carefully carried Elora's molds out the door.

I sank back into the rocking chair next to Travis, relieved to have some time to think and process without anyone else in the room. But Lisa had only been gone a minute when Dr. Moon came back with a member of the organ donation team.

The conversation was short. The representative said he'd reviewed Elora's file. "We've determined that due to the extensive damage to her organs and the possibility that her tumor could be cancerous, Elora is not a likely candidate for donation."

Organ donation had offered the solace of a higher purpose, a reason to let Elora go that made sense. Without it, I was left holding "whys" that had no answers.

Dr. Moon added, "The results from Elora's biopsy haven't come back yet, so we don't know whether the tumor is cancerous. Let's put this on hold for now, and if you want to re-evaluate later, we can do that."

The representative handed brochures to both of us in case we had any questions. Travis only had one.

"If we can't donate Elora's organs, then what?"

Dr. Moon leaned forward in her chair, reaching across the doctor/patient divide with compassionate eyes. "If organ donation isn't possible for Elora, there will be a different decision for you to make." She cleared her throat as her professional demeanor slipped momentarily. "You can keep Elora on the ventilator and her organs will shut down on their own sometime over the next several days. Or you can choose to take her off life support."

I sat like a statue. Vacant. Numb. Staring at the cover of the pamphlet in my hand, the slick paper sticking to my clammy fingers.

Choose?

My stomach soured, and my head floated into thin air. I couldn't breathe. Every muscle clenched in revulsion. Since when was this decision up to me? Wasn't God supposed to be in charge? How had the end of Elora's life been shifted to my shoulders?

Choose?

That choice was like staring at two bottles of poison and deciding which I'd rather drink.

One choice would prolong Elora's suffering.

The other would take her away from me even faster.

How is that a choice? There's no way to make it!

The only thing I knew for certain was I wanted no part in deciding how Elora would leave her life. I wouldn't do it.

Dr. Moon handed Travis the do-not-resuscitate order, then she and the organ donation representative left to give us time to think. Snippets of information swirled around my head, mixing, tangling, throbbing behind my eyes until they burned like fever.

Travis dug a pen out of his laptop bag and scribbled his signature across a black line at the bottom of the paper in his hand. He passed it to me. I signed it. And then I panicked.

Do not resuscitate. Organ donation. Life support.

Elora's life in my hands. In my exhausted, sleep-deprived, stress-addled hands. What if I got it wrong? What if there was still a miracle God wanted to send, but I couldn't hear it through the muddle in my mind?

I blurted out, "Trav, I can't do this. I'm past exhausted, and I can't think straight. Everything hurts so much!" I started to cry, but I was so tired of crying that I made myself stop. "I don't trust myself to make any more decisions about Elora while I'm in this condition."

Travis reached over and took the pen and paper from my hands. "How can I help?"

His eyes were bloodshot. Stubble covered his chin, and stress creased his forehead. "Babe, you're exhausted too," I said. "We need to sleep. Just for a little bit. Before we make any more decisions."

He nodded. "I think we could both use a break."

At the nurses' station, I asked to use one of the sleeping rooms connected to the PICU waiting room. A nurse handed me the key to door #3. I hated leaving Elora, hated trading time at her side for time asleep, but I'd hit a wall. My body and mind were shutting down. I was desperate for answers about Elora, and I couldn't keep my thoughts sorted long enough to hear if God was giving them to me.

The PICU waiting room was dark again for the evening. Travis and I navigated the room by the blue light of the fish tank. The previously filled room was empty except for my parents who were settled on a couch with Noah asleep in his car seat at their feet, another empty bottle at his side. At least he wasn't hungry, and bottle feeding had made it easier on everyone caring for him.

But the separation wasn't fair. To him or me.

I crouched down and softly stroked Noah's downy eyebrow with one finger, trying to connect without waking him.

Mom looked at Travis and said, "Kathy wanted you to know that she's gone to help get your kids settled, but she'll be back soon." Travis nodded his thanks.

The key to room #3 still dangled from my finger. My parents had come into the dark waiting room to try to rest, but they were the only ones left in the hospital and I wouldn't be able to sleep knowing Elora was alone.

I took my mom's hand. "Could you guys go sit with Elora? Travis and I have got to try to sleep or…" The sentence wouldn't finish.

Mom stood up from the couch and slung the diaper bag over her arm. "Of course we'll sit with her. We'd be honored."

Dad lifted Noah's seat. "You guys go and rest."

"Promise you'll come get me right away if anything happens? *Anything.*" I swallowed down another surge of panic, too exhausted to cry.

"We promise." Mom covered Noah's seat with his blanket.

"Krista. Rest." I could never argue with Dad's loving-stern voice. He held the door open for Mom, and they disappeared into the bright hallway.

The sleeping room was basically a long closet with white walls and one twin-sized bed. Travis insisted I use it, promising he'd be perfectly comfortable on one of the waiting room couches. I kissed him and let the heavy door swing itself closed as I kicked off my shoes. I took out my ponytail, turned off the light, and felt my way blindly to the bed. The sheets smelled freshly washed and the wool blanket was just heavy enough to provide instant warmth. But without Elora's whirring machines, the flow of visitors, and Travis's voice, the quiet in the room was deafening.

My body begged for the oblivion of sleep, my limbs impossibly heavy, but my mind blared like a siren. Incoherent streams of pictures, colors, shapes, and madness collided behind my eyelids. I rolled over and pushed my face into the pillow. I lost track of time while I struggled to let go, but after muttering a prayer asking God that nothing would happen to Elora while I slept, my mind finally relented and went completely dark.

Sometime later, I awoke sharply with a jolt.

There'd been a nightmare.

One of my kids in the hospital.

Sick.

So vivid I could still hear the beeping and whirring of the machines.

Petrifying.

I reached out for Travis's chest, but the edge of the bed was in the wrong place and the sheets were stiff cotton, not flannel.

Where am I?

The room was too dark, the jaundiced glow of my bedroom alarm clock missing. I sat up and noticed a thin line of blue light bruising the floor. I knew that light. It matched the color of the fish tank in my dream. The fish tank in the waiting room at the hospital.

No.

Not a nightmare. Real. It was all real.

Elora.

I laid my head slowly backward into the pillow, hid my face with the blanket, and dripped salty tears into the wounds of my rediscovered grief.

"And he went a little further, and fell on his face, and prayed, saying, O my Father, if it be possible, let this cup pass from me: nevertheless not as I will, but as thou wilt."

MATTHEW 26:39

18

NOT MY WILL

lora.

Engulfed by the anonymity of the pitch-black room, I pressed the blanket to my face, wetting it through with fresh grief.

Why is this real? Why Elora?

Despair overtook me entirely until a sudden realization jolted me upright just as my nightmare had.

How long was I asleep?

Judging by how tired I still felt, it was a short time, but my body was so far off normal that I couldn't be sure.

What if it's been way longer than I think?

The blue light under the door meant it was still night.

But what if something happened to Elora and no one knew where to find me? An emergency. What if they couldn't spare anyone to come get me?

Manic fear shot through my veins as I scrambled from the bed, fumbling blindly forward with both hands toward the wall. I slapped at the rough surface until I hit the light switch, then shoved my feet into my shoes, grabbed my cell phone and sweatshirt off the floor, and threw open the door.

The waiting room appeared the same as I'd left it—silent and still but for the oblivious fish swirling in tranquil fluorescence. But Travis wasn't there.

Maybe he's with Elora.

I ran for the door that led to the hallway. I had to get to Elora. Make sure she was all right. I was steps away when Mom and Dad opened the door.

"Elora!" I shouted at them. "Is she…? What happened?"

They hadn't seen me running at them through the shadows and stepped back in surprise.

"Honey," Mom soothed, running her hands down my arms. "Everything's fine. She's fine."

"But how long was I out? What time is it?"

Mom looked at her watch. "It's just after midnight. You only slept for a couple of hours."

Dad set baby Noah in his car seat on the floor and rubbed my shoulder. "Mom and I were with her the whole time."

Mom nodded. "Kathy is with her now. She said she'd take a turn sitting with Elora so we could rest."

Despite their assurances, my heartbeat pulsed in my neck and fingertips. My heart would not be fully appeased until I saw Elora with my own eyes. "You guys okay if I go?"

"Yes, honey, go. Dad and I are going to try to sleep a little," Mom said. "But it was a privilege to sit with Elora."

I hugged them both, walked between them, grasped the doorknob, but turned back. "Did either of you see Trav?"

"He went for a walk," Dad said. "He couldn't sleep."

"Okay. I'll try calling him. Thanks."

I jogged down the hall to the PICU doors, buzzed myself in,

rushed past the nurses' station, and burst into Elora's room. A nurse with long blonde hair stood on one side of the bed. My mother-in-law, Kathy, stood on the other side, holding Elora's hand.

The room was calm.

Elora was still alive.

I still have time.

I leaned forward across the end of the bed to steady myself and cradled Elora's feet under my chin. She smelled of...

Baby powder?

Kathy reached out and stroked the top of my head. "Hey, sweetie. Did you get some rest?"

"Yeah, I slept. Not enough, but I can't stand being away any longer. Thanks for staying."

"Oh, well, this is the most important place to be in the world right now." The soft lights behind Elora's bed glowed around Kathy's head, illuminating subtle red highlights in her elbow-length auburn hair. Elora had definitely inherited her grandmother's beautiful locks.

"Anything happen while I was gone? Any changes?"

"Oh, Krista, you won't believe how much love this little girl has received while you were gone."

"Really? What happened?"

"The nurses gave her the sweetest little sponge bath and even brushed her teeth with a tiny sponge on a stick..." I stood up and looked at Elora more carefully. The flecks of blood and iodine from the surgery were gone, leaving her face clean and fresh. "Then your mom and I rubbed her with baby lotion before the nurses put her in clean pajamas..."

Ah...baby powder...

"And Monique here has spent the last hour washing and combing out her hair."

I moved around the edge of the bed to inspect the results of Nurse Monique's work and gasped at the transformation. Armed with a bottle of detangling spray and a comb, Monique had patiently coaxed Elora's blood-matted tangle into a single auburn ponytail draped over her left shoulder. I ran my fingers through the silky strands.

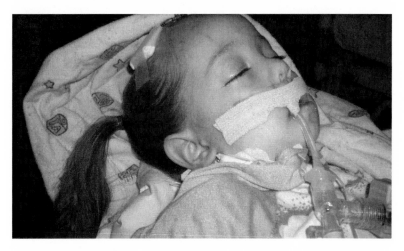

Elora's remaining hair, post-surgery,
washed and combed into a ponytail by Nurse Monique
January 19, 2007

I put my arm around Monique in a side hug. "I thought that little bit of hair was ruined. I didn't think I'd ever see it like this again. You don't know what it means. Thank you."

Monique hugged me back and wiped her eyes. "It was my pleasure to spend time with your sweet little girl."

Suddenly, Monique stood bolt upright and pulled away from our hug. "I almost forgot! I have a couple of things for you," she said. "First, Elora's hand and foot castings came back." She lifted two white plaster replicas from the counter behind us and placed them in my hands. The detail truly was amazing— the evidence of fingernail polish, the bumps on Elora's sucking fingers, the shape of her toes.

"Mom, look at these." Kathy took the castings from me and examined every crease and pore.

Next, Monique held out a cream-colored linen box. The double-flapped lid was tied closed in the middle with a green ribbon. I untied the ribbon and opened the flaps. The box was divided into small compartments, each labeled with a memento it could hold. In the largest section was a clear medical bag filled with several clumps of auburn hair.

"It's a memory box. A gift from the hospital," Monique said.

"But the hair. Where…?"

"I went back into the operating room once they brought Elora to us and gathered up as much hair as I could. I thought you might want it."

I hugged her again and cried on her shoulder. This woman I'd never met had gone out of her way to serve and bless me in ways only she could.

Monique had another patient to attend to, but she promised to check in with us again soon. I moved next to Kathy to sit in my usual chair, but I felt too restless to sit. I held the plaster castings next to Elora's hand and foot, comparing the details. They were beautiful, near perfect replicas. But I was not ready for plaster to replace flesh, and my last conversation with Dr. Moon crept to the forefront of my thoughts.

Let Elora's organs fail on their own over the next several days or remove her from life support.

An impossible decision.

Letting her pass on her own would be easier in some ways because I would have days more to be with her, touch her skin, smother her with kisses, and *see* her. Then God would be responsible for the moment she would leave this earth, not me. But it would also require Elora to suffer for days in pain, and I would have to suffer the witnessing of that.

Removing life support was the kinder choice because she would be freed from the pain of her broken body. I could take the reins from God, give the command, and it would be carried out immediately. Never to touch her or kiss her again my entire life. How could I give away the last days I would ever spend with her? How could I stand at her side and speak the words that would end her life? Never. I could never do it. I would rather die myself.

My decision was *not* to decide. I tried to go back to simply spending time at Elora's side, but the question stalked me as I paced the floor, pressed on me if I tried to sit still, nagged at me, pestered me as I stared at her precious face.

I had boarded a ship in a storm, tumbling from one edge of the deck to the other, back and forth as the waves rose and fell. I could not stand firmly on either side.

God had placed Elora's life in my hands and I could not escape the responsibility, no matter how hard I tried. In the end, not deciding was still deciding. And was that really what God wanted me to do? It was impossible to know which action to take, at least without His help. But for the first time in my life, I was afraid to ask Him what I should do. If I prayed, I was certain He would give me an answer, but I didn't know if I was ready to hear it. What if He asked what I wasn't prepared to do?

Heavenly Father, please don't make me choose. Seeing Elora in pain like this is agony, but taking her off life support would be too. Either way, I lose her. Please don't make me be the one who has to choose how her life ends! I can't bear to have any part in that.

I needed Travis. Needed him to talk me through this. My cell phone didn't have great reception in the PICU, but I dialed his number anyway. It went straight to voicemail.

Where is he?

I redialed and redialed, pacing in a tight circle at the foot of Elora's bed. Kathy noticed my agitation. "What's wrong?"

"Trav's not answering his phone. Did he tell you where he was going?"

"No, but he won't stay away from Elora or you for long. I'm sure he'll be back soon."

I forced myself into a chair, intent on losing myself in the pleasure of holding Elora's hand while I still could, but the smallness of her fingers curled in my palm only worsened the ache in my heart for the decision roiling oppressively on my horizon, raising the hair on the back of my neck, striking lightning fear into my core until all I wanted was to run.

Kathy tried to distract me with questions about my kids and news about the family and I did my best to listen and answer, but I couldn't concentrate. I dialed Travis's phone again and again. Finally, he came in through the door and wrapped his arms around me.

"Where have you been?" I asked.

He whispered in my ear, the stubble on his chin prickling my cheek. "I went for a walk and to pray. You and I need to talk."

"I know."

"Come with me."

"Where?"

"Outside."

I turned around so I could read his face. Dark rings circling his eyes betrayed his exhaustion, and yet, as I looked into their familiar brown depths, there was a hint of resolution, of peace. "You know, don't you?" I asked.

"What?"

"The answer. What we should do."

He hesitated. "Yes. Please come with me."

Kathy agreed to stay with Elora. Travis and I left the PICU, rode the elevator down to the main lobby, and walked out the front door past a little tinkling fountain filled with wishing pennies. How I hoped that each of those coins represented another person's wish granted, even if all the pennies in the world could not give me mine.

The night air was chilly, but the sky was clear. Travis pulled me close, and we both tipped our heads back to look at the stars. Nothing between us and God.

"What did God tell you? When you prayed," I asked him.

"I can't tell you."

"Why not?"

"Because...you need to find out for yourself."

I didn't like it. It would be so much easier to be told what to do.

"I don't want to," I said, choking on the emotional pressure building in my heart and throat.

"I know you don't," Travis said, "but if you don't find out for yourself, you'll never really know if we made the right decision. And I'm afraid of what that would do to you."

Travis was right. He could tell me his decision, but without knowing for myself that it was God's will, I would never be at peace. I might even blame him one day, and I didn't want that. This needed to be a mutual decision made by both of us. Independently equal.

"Will you say the prayer for me?" I asked.

"No. Sweetheart, you need to do this."

"But I don't know if I can! I have a feeling about what He's going to ask us to do." I started to cry. "And I don't know if I can do it!"

Travis pressed his cheek to mine. "I know. But I'll be right here with you."

We moved a bit farther off the path to be sure we were alone. Then with my hands folded between my husband's and my head bowed beneath the infinite cosmos, I began a most desperate petition to God. I spoke aloud, letting my words bleed raw and unbandaged.

"Dear Father in Heaven, I don't know what to do. I know you're going to take my girl, and it hurts so badly. I'm so scared. I don't *want* her to go. I want her to stay here with me even though I know she can't anymore."

Lips quivering, raging tears, running nose, and ragged breath tearing at my chest, I continued, "Father? If you need to take her home, then take her. I know she'll be safe with you, and I'll see her again when I get there. But this choosing thing? I can't do it. It's the most terrible thing you could ask me to do. I don't want to decide when she goes. I want you to do it. Please don't make me be the one to give up on her. Don't ask me to say those words. It will kill me. Will you please just take her? Please, *please*…don't make me choose."

Instantly, there were words in my head. Hundreds of them

pouring like a river into my desert soul all at the same time, tumbling over one another in a flash flood of inspiration, and yet I understood them. They were familiar to me. Snippets of an answer God had foreseen I would need and prepared in advance of my most desperate prayer.

Two weeks previously during my usual morning scripture study, I was struck with a desire to understand how Jesus had so humbly submitted His will to God's, knowing it would cause Him so much pain. I was filled with an insatiable desire to study everything I could find on the subject. For two weeks, I devoured scriptures under headings like "Trust in God," "Will," and "Agency," and when I had exhausted topics in the scriptures, I hunted for additional talks and articles written by church leaders. The study was as delicious to me as a feast, and the morning before Elora got sick, I said to Travis, "I don't know what it is about this topic, but I can't get enough."

God knew. He'd known all along about Elora's tumor and that I would be faced with this decision. He knew that I would offer this exact prayer, and that the words He had prompted me to study, fresh in my mind, would strengthen me and help me to hear His will.

I heard Him.

God's words in my mind spoke directly to me in my moment of greatest need. Words that said He loved me. Words that promised peace. Blessings for following His will. Reassurance that He never abandons His children.

I stood silently in the middle of my prayer, allowing God to speak to me. Travis stood reverently, unmoving, letting me experience what he could not see or hear himself.

I listened to the flood of God's words, and through them, I

understood His will for me, for Elora. He was asking me to do the very thing I feared most.

I opened my eyes without ending the prayer and cried out to Travis, "I know what He wants us to do, but I don't think I can."

"What did He say?"

"To tell the doctor to take her off life support."

"That's what He told me too."

I broke. Fear, agony, and despair smeared and dripped from my soaked face and burned in my throat as I wailed from depths of dread into the cold midnight air. Not caring if anyone heard. Knowing God would.

"How? Travis, I can't!"

"I know. Honey, I know." His face was screwed and twisted in misery.

I prayed again, only silently this time so only God would hear.

Father, how? Why? It's the worst thing you could ask me to do! It's cruel! I don't understand! How can that be what you want?

I stood at a crossroads. I could refuse God and walk away—tell Him I wasn't strong enough. Or I could continue to trust my Father in Heaven, even though I did not understand His will.

If I'd learned anything from my study, it was that God had asked Jesus to do something even harder than this, and Jesus had done it because He trusted His Father. It had hurt Him—pain greater than anyone could understand. But Christ's humility and faith led Him through the Atonement—a *blessing* greater than anyone could understand.

God had proven Himself to me over and over since Elora's first seizure. He had prepared my way and put blessings along my path even before I knew I would need them. As long as I held to Him, He had given me the strength to endure *everything* to this point. He had not abandoned me. So, how could I abandon Him now? How could I turn my back on the very source of my preservation?

The stars shone down clear and bright as I reached my hand heavenward once more, unclenched my heart, released the vise of my will, and placed it all on God's altar.

Father, this is the worst thing you've ever asked me to do, and I still don't know how I'm going to do it, but I trust you. I don't understand it, but I have faith that you can see things I can't.

Warmth spread through my chest, but my body shook with all-consuming fear and exhaustion. I was incapable of going any further without help.

I'll do what you ask, but if you want me to walk into that hospital and tell the doctor this decision, you're going to have to help me because I don't have the strength left to do it.

I don't know in what form I expected His help to come, but suddenly, there were arms, unseen arms surrounding me. Strong, warm, and filled with indescribable love. They wrapped around my shoulders, my arms, my back. Angels—family or friends passed on from this earth—or the Savior Himself, I could not say. But whoever was with me loved me immensely and had come to strengthen me through this final act.

"Trav? If we're going to do this, we have to go now or I might change my mind and lie down right here and never get up again."

He interlocked his fingers with mine.

Then those magnificent unseen arms propelled me past the wishing fountain and toward the front doors of the hospital.

19

THE EDGE OF HEAVEN

$\mathcal{J}$ RE-ENTERED THE HOSPITAL with Travis at my side. The elevators were directly ahead, across the lobby, and I focused on them like a drained marathoner, urging my legs to make it at least that far. With each step, my dread grew. God was assisting me, I had no doubt, but I still couldn't imagine my tongue forming the words that would end Elora's life. Every step closer to that elevator meant one second closer to a goodbye that would last my entire life.

"Krista?"

Travis and I were halfway to the elevators, and though I was vaguely aware of other people in the lobby, I hadn't paid them any attention. I shifted my gaze to a woman approaching in the dim lighting.

"Heidi?" An old friend and neighbor. I'd forgotten she worked at the hospital.

"Yeah, it's me. Honey, what are you doing here? What's wrong?" She wrapped me in a fierce hug.

"I'm going upstairs right now to tell the doctor to take my Elora off life support."

I'd said it.

Out loud.

The words had just come. My friend, in the right place, at the right time, asking just the right question for me to have a miraculous practice session.

"What? Krista…. I…."

"I know. I need to go now." There was nothing else I could say, and my strength might have failed if I'd tried. She hugged me tighter, then let me go, but remained frozen with shock, watching me until the elevator doors closed.

The walk to Elora's room was a blur. I leaned heavily against those unseen arms surrounding me. Travis and I stopped by the PICU waiting room to ask my parents to bring Noah and join us. Travis's mom, Kathy, was still sitting with Elora. We told our parents our decision, and everyone cried as Travis pressed the nurse call button beside Elora's bed. "Can we speak with Dr. Moon, please?"

Elora lay before me, warm, and real, and tangible. Almost every night over the past several months, she had crawled out of her bed and crept into my room. It was the sucking of the fingers that always gave her away and woke me up.

"Come in, Elora," I'd say, then she would climb up the foot of my bed and crawl to the middle, right between me and Travis.

How could I go home without her? See her toys, her clothes, her shoes where she'd left them.

How would I ever be whole again with her missing?

I half-climbed onto the bed, as close to Elora as possible, and whispered so only she would hear. "Baby girl, Daddy and I have decided that it's time for us to let you go." Great drops of my sorrow fell onto her cheek. I wiped them away gently, but more fell. "I think you've been ready for a while now, but it was really hard for me to see that. I can't stand being without you, but I don't want you to hurt anymore."

There was one more thing I needed to say before I could truly let her go, one thing that would haunt me forever if I didn't ask it. "Baby, please forgive me for not knowing how much you were hurting. Forgive me for not figuring it out sooner. I promise to do whatever it takes to make it to where you're going. And then I'll hug you so hard for so long. I promise. I love you forever and ever."

The door opened, and Dr. Moon walked to the end of the bed. "The nurses said you were looking for me?"

I stood upright, my body shaking uncontrollably. Travis nodded my way, signaling that I should be the one to say the words. It was a task that, up until that second, I would have resisted. But as I stood trembling at Elora's side, my memories flew to another day in another hospital that was also filled with great personal pain. Her birth day. And at last, I understood why I needed to be the one to say the words.

Who else should experience the greatest pain of helping her out of this world except the woman who willingly experienced the great pain of bringing her here? I was her mother. The privilege of that pain was mine.

God, please give me one more second of courage.

"Dr. Moon." My voice trembled worse than my body. "We've made the decision to take Elora off life support."

Instantly, a warmth touched the crown of my head and flowed downward like a waterfall of peace breaking over my scalp. The tranquil sensation coursed over my shoulders and down my back, through my stomach and into my legs. I closed my eyes as the tremors eased from my body. When it reached the tips of my toes, I opened my eyes and smiled at Travis. "That's right. That's the right decision. Isn't it?"

Travis smiled back through his tears. "Yes, it is," he said.

A peaceful spirit permeated the room, confirming to everyone that it was indeed the right decision.

Dr. Moon reached out and took my hand, her own mother-heart spilling tears of sympathy. "You've made the right decision. That's exactly what I would do in your place." All along she'd been generously holding back her opinion, letting us find peace in our own answers, process them in our own way, at our own speed. She wiped her eyes before stepping to the doorway and summoning a nurse. In a hushed conversation that I could not hear, Dr. Moon issued instructions. The nurse listened intently, nodding every few seconds, and then Dr. Moon turned back to us. "They'll be right in." She held my gaze, a moment of shared tears, then she left.

Three nurses, including Monique, entered the room. One took a moment to respectfully explain the process of unhooking Elora from all of the machines so we would know what to expect. First the non-vital machines, such as the heart monitor, would be shut off and removed. Next, Elora would be given one last dose of morphine through her IV to ensure she didn't feel pain. Then the vital tubes, wires, and drains would be removed until only her breathing tube was left. That would be last.

Travis and I signed our consent on a form, and the process began.

The nurses worked with great care and reverence, delicately unencumbering Elora from the machines tethering her to this world.

Once again, my body was taken over by tremors.

Will she feel anything? What if she opens her eyes, or gasps for breath, or struggles?

I was petrified.

Heavenly Father, please let us be strong enough to watch her die.

One by one, the beeping, whirring machines quieted, leaving only the stuttered whimpers of our grieving family and the whoosh of the final machine pressing numbered breaths in and out of Elora's lungs.

Monique guided Travis to stand facing me. She draped a soft blanket over our outstretched arms, then the three nurses coordinated lifting Elora from the bed into our combined embrace. Travis and I cradled her between our stricken hearts, sobbing out our enduring love for her, with promises of togetherness in the next life. Our parents stood looking on in tormented grief.

Then, "One, two, three." A nurse pulled Elora's breathing tube from her throat, and the nurses left the room.

Travis and I clung to our girl, pulling each other more tightly together around her. I watched the life drain from her—mercifully, she did not struggle—but when her lips turned blue, I knew she was gone.

My sorrow ran wild, raw, unashamed. I sobbed until every molecule of my soul ached with the pain of it.

Heaven lay just beyond my sight. There were more people in that room than I could see. Travis and I had walked to the edge of heaven, and reaching through the veil, we passed Elora into the arms of loved ones on the other side.

I felt them come for her.

I asked them to watch over her until the day I was reunited with her there.

Travis had me sit in the rocking chair and hold Elora by myself. I rocked her, wrapped tightly in the blanket, free from IVs and monitors and drainage lines and breathing tubes and taped lips. I stroked and kissed her perfect face without any obstruction. The air around us grew sacred while I choked out her favorite lullaby one last time. And in that moment, holding Elora's body freely in my arms, with Travis and our parents in the room, I finally understood why God had asked me to trust His will and choose to remove Elora from life support.

If God had taken Elora home at some random time, like I asked, there was no guarantee that Travis or I would have been in the room when she died, let alone together and with our parents. And even if by some miracle we *were* together, Elora would have died beneath all of that equipment in a cold bed. At most, I might have been holding her hand.

I could see it now.

What I had viewed as cruelty was really a loving invitation for us to accompany Elora, warm in our arms, as she passed over the threshold of heaven.

God knew that it would forever be the most excruciatingly sacred moment of my life. He hadn't forced me to obey. He would have respected my agency if I'd chosen the other path. But as I rocked Elora for the last time, I realized what I would have missed if I hadn't listened, if I hadn't trusted Him.

I finished Elora's lullaby just as a nurse with a stethoscope came to confirm her passing. He marked her death at 2:00 am, January 20th, 2007. It was Saturday. A mere thirty hours since that first seizure that had eternally changed my world.

"I'm so sorry for your loss," the nurse said, then left us alone again.

I kissed Elora's forehead and took one last, long breath of her, then lifted her for Travis to hold. He wrapped her in his strong arms, buried his face in her neck, and roared out his mourning. I couldn't bear it. Witnessing his absolute pain was worse than my own despair. For a moment I looked away, but could not escape the sound. My heart's wound was torn more deeply for the pain of my husband. His voice soon softened and turned to whispers in Elora's ear, and then with the greatest gentleness, he laid her down on the bed.

Kathy and my parents took turns kissing her and whispering their own heartbroken farewells, then we opened the door. The nurses returned, no longer restraining their sorrow, and began to gently arrange Elora. They propped her head on a soft pillow, tucked the sheet and blanket warmly over her chest, and straightened her ponytail down her shoulder. I watched for a moment, but then couldn't anymore. I didn't want to wait for them to take her away. I wanted to leave with the melody of her lullaby on my tongue and the faint scent of baby powder in the air.

Outside Elora's room, in front of the PICU nurse's station, I embraced every nurse and Dr. Moon and thanked them for their tender care of Elora and our whole family. They wept with me.

Nurse Monique brought me the keepsake box with Elora's hair inside, the plaster hand and foot castings wrapped in protective paper, a teddy bear that Travis's cousin had sent to the room, the blanket Elora had used in the PICU, several coloring pages that Shaustia had done to brighten the room, and finally, Elora's hospital tags freshly cut from her wrist. I hugged Monique before she returned to her duties in Elora's room, and as the door slowly swung closed behind her, I stole one final glance of my precious girl and walked away.

Fear thou not; for I am with thee: be not dismayed;
for I am thy God: I will strengthen thee;
yea, I will help thee; yea, I will uphold thee
with the right hand of my righteousness.

ISAIAH 41:10

20

HOME

No one stopped me from leaving the PICU. I waited in the hallway alone, in a stupor, stutter-breathed from crying too hard.

How is this real? How is Elora gone?

Reality spun in my head like a website that couldn't load.

Disconnected.

No answers.

Disbelief. Numbness. Shock.

Kathy, and my parents, carrying Noah, joined me in the hall, all of them red-eyed, wiping their faces.

Travis was last. He wanted to be sure his kiss was the final one on Elora's cheek.

We stood speechless together, waiting for someone to tell us what to do next. But no one came. Travis asked, "Are we supposed to stay? Or do we just go home?"

Home.

Going home was supposed to be a celebration of Elora's recovery, our world returning to normal. Elora was supposed to be with me. Awake and smiling. In my arms. But now going ne meant leaving her behind. Turning my back. Walking away. Driving to a home that would never again have her in it.

A longing ache crept into my chest, seeping like wet cement into the trauma-induced fissures of Elora's loss. An ache that would soon set hard and permanent. Elora would always be missing. Every day for the rest of my life. That would never change, no matter how long I stood in that hallway.

Kathy and my mom agreed that if there was anything more the hospital needed from us, they knew how to reach us.

In bleary half-awareness, I followed Mom back to the darkened waiting room to gather our belongings. Shock fogged my thoughts, slowed my body, and shivered in my hands and knees, but as long as I kept moving, I managed to stay just ahead of its full consumption.

Once Mom and I had all of our bags, I took one last envious look at the oblivious fish swirling in their tank, then turned my back and left them behind for good.

In the brightness of the hallway, I fussed with the diaper bag, searching for phantom belongings, checking and rechecking the items Monique had brought from Elora's room, unclear if I was missing anything since I couldn't keep track of any of it or remember what we'd brought with us in the first place.

I couldn't stop. Fussing, fiddling, moving. It was all I could do to stay distracted, one step ahead of the despair lapping at my heels.

Not here. Wait until home.

Travis took the diaper bag from my shoulder and handed it to Kathy. Dad carried Noah in his car seat, and Mom carried the plastic sack of Elora's things. Travis carried his laptop bag and held my hand.

No one said a thing. We just aimed ourselves down the hall, toward the elevator.

I clung to Travis's arm as together we plodded one last time across the hospital lobby, out the main doors, past the disenchanted wish fountain to the parking garage. Kathy and my parents had their own cars, but they helped us load all of our things and secure Noah's car seat before we split up.

Travis's weariness overwhelmed him as soon as we left the parking lot, so he drove to the nearest gas station to buy a soda. I waited in the car with sleeping Noah. The sky on the horizon above the mountains had just begun to fade from inky black to hazy gray, dimming the brightness of the stars. I watched the earliest signs of a new day, heartsick that the world would soon awaken and start asking questions. All those sleeping people who had prayed for Elora in their bedtime prayers, still unaware that she was gone. The sun would rise and so would they, and I would have to tell them what had happened.

And that would make it real.

The diaper bag rested at my feet, a small corner of green-striped cloth sticking out of the top. I pulled the shirt from the bag and searched for the dark spot on the right sleeve. I had run from my home less than two days before with Elora swaddled in that shirt, held against my chest, no idea that this spot of her blood and a tangle of her hair in a baggie would be the only part of her I'd be bringing home.

I rubbed the stained fibers between my thumb and forefinger, swearing never to wash away that evidence that she had really lived, that she had once been mine.

Travis downed his soda as we took the onramp to the freeway, but even with an entire caffeinated beverage in his system, he couldn't keep his eyes open. He pulled off on the weedy shoulder of the freeway so we could trade places. He laid the passenger seat back as far as it would go and fell asleep instantly. I drove toward home, eyes on the dying night sky, one hand on the steering wheel, the other on Travis's chest. Silence but for the hum of the van's engine and the deafening collapse of my world as I'd known it.

Thirty minutes later, the tires bounced over the curb of our driveway. The last time they'd made that sound, Elora was asleep in her car seat, and I'd carried her safely into the house. I glanced through the rearview mirror at her excruciatingly empty seat. Half of me wanted to tear it from the van and hurl it into the street. The other half wanted to leave it in that exact spot for eternity—crushed Cheerios, stale French fries, and all.

I turned off the ignition and exhaled slowly. Travis woke and sat his seat upright, but neither of us moved to go into the house. We just sat, staring ahead, both afraid to cross the threshold of our new normal.

Mom, Dad, and Kathy arrived, parking their cars in the driveway behind us just as Noah woke up and cried to be fed. Instinctually my hand reached for the handle and opened the door. Ready or not, it was time.

Travis unloaded our bags as I unloaded Noah. Cradling him in one arm, I walked up the cement steps to the garage door and stepped into a house still shrouded in early morning silence. The clock on the microwave read 3:30 a.m. The dishes were washed and the front room was spotless, but as promised, everyone had left Elora's things exactly as she'd left them.

While Travis helped Mom and Dad bring in their luggage, I wandered the rooms like a ghost, observing the final placements of Elora's life.

Her favorite Winnie the Pooh shoes and a pair of dirty white socks by the front door.

The fluffy white coat given to her as a Christmas gift hung in the laundry room with a chocolate-milk stain dribbled down the front.

A pink sippy cup against the baseboard in the hallway, half-filled with curdled milk.

Her bed, still unmade, covered in a mound of sheets and blankets I'd washed after she was sick on them.

Dolls, plastic princess high heels, crayons, and her stuffed duck dotted her bedroom floor, as well as a few wrappers from candy she'd snuck without asking.

Downstairs in the basement, several relatives slept on couches and floors. Jared and his wife, Jenn, had brought Caleb, Shaustia, and Walker home and put them to bed. My heart wanted to scoop up my children, cover their faces in kisses, and never let them go, but they slept so peacefully, I didn't dare disturb their final night of sweet dreams before telling them about Elora.

Jared and Jenn woke with the noise of luggage and whispered conversation and came upstairs, the first to ask news of Elora. Travis and I and our parents sat in the front room with them and told the story of Elora's passing, christening our home with the first tears of mourning.

As pale rays of earliest sunlight peeked through the living room blinds, Kathy stood to collect her coat and purse.

"Mom," Travis said, "are you okay to drive? I'm worried about you being so tired. You can stay here tonight."

She slipped her arms into her coat. "I'll be just fine. It's only fifteen minutes, and I'll sleep better in my own bed." She kissed

Travis, then me. "I'll start spreading the word to family tomorrow, and I'll be back later in the day to help with the kids, or whatever else you need."

Travis put on his shoes and held her arm all the way out to her car.

I chatted with Jared and Jenn for a few more minutes, but as I sat on the couch, the last of the adrenaline that had kept me going over the past thirty hours drained away, leaving me in desperate need of rest. Travis too.

And Mom could see that.

In that moment, she appointed herself guardian and gatekeeper of our care and ordered us to bed. We obeyed.

But before I closed my bedroom door, I had one last request.

"Mom, please don't let anyone tell the kids about Elora. Travis and I want to be the ones to do that."

"I'll do my best." She rubbed my arm in the gentle way she always did, and I closed the door between us.

Travis turned down the covers of our bed while I changed into my softest flannel pajamas. We both crawled to Elora's spot in the middle of our mattress, holding each other tightly. But my body had been fighting extreme, traumatic exhaustion for so long, every muscle throbbed, and sleep proved elusive.

In the quiet stillness that had forced me to stop running, despair finally caught up, colliding with my soul like a flash flood.

I let go. And let it wash me away.

I cried and cried and cried. My stomach muscles cramped from the exertion, and my face tingled from lack of breath, but still I cried, great tears dripping rhythmically onto my pillow.

Missing. Missing. Missing.

I kept waiting to hear the door crack open, the swish of a

diaper, and sucking fingers waiting for permission to crawl into the bed.

Missing. Missing. Missing.

I needed her in the middle, someway, somehow. I unwrapped myself from Travis's embrace, crept to the laundry room, fished through a laundry basket of clean clothes, and returned to my room.

Travis cried too as I smoothed Elora's yellow sunflower pajamas over the sheet between us. We both lay facing them, one hand each resting where her stomach should have been. I closed my eyes, the well-worn seersucker fabric beneath my fingers, and cried until exhaustion finally won out.

Thou shalt live together in love,
insomuch that thou shalt weep for the loss
of them that die . . .

DOCTRINE AND COVENANTS 42:45

21

ALL MINE

MY HAND STILL RESTED next to Travis's on Elora's pajamas when I woke. I had temporarily escaped my despair in the depths of sleep, but as I opened my eyes, I could feel it rushing toward me once more.

My body ached terribly, and the raw skin on my face burned. I didn't want to cry anymore, but my heart didn't care what my body wanted.

I attempted to sob quietly, but could not restrain the sorrow that pressed painfully through my body, shaking the mattress and waking Travis. He held my hand and let me cry myself out until an unbearable headache gave my grief momentary pause.

I needed pain medicine and to use the restroom, but my body felt too heavy to move. I rolled onto my back and pushed one leg over the edge of the mattress, letting it dangle in the air. After a minute, I pushed the other leg out of bed. Finally, I forced myself upright and planted my feet on the floor, leaning heavily against the edge of the mattress.

My usual morning routine involved kneeling beside my bed in prayer, but I knew God would understand if today I stood.

Father, the only way I'm going to make it through today is with your help. Please stay with me.

Then I took the first tremendously laden step into my first day without Elora.

After the restroom, I sipped faucet water from my cupped hand to swallow two ibuprofen, then looked at myself in the mirror for the first time in days. My dirty, knotted blonde hair stood at odd angles, my eyelids had swollen partly shut around my bloodshot eyes, and the skin on my cheeks, nose, and upper lip blared painfully red, raw, and flaky.

I splashed some cold water on my face to soothe literal salt from my wounds, corralled my hair into a messy ponytail, wrapped my bathrobe over my pajamas, and barely had the strength to make it onto a barstool at the kitchen island.

The countertop was covered with food. Stacks of waffles and ebelskiver pancake balls, homemade strawberry jam in a glass canning jar, fresh fruit arranged on an unfamiliar platter, juices, chocolate milk, and a plate of warm bacon.

Mom took a break from clearing the kids' used breakfast dishes from the table to greet me with a long hug. "Apparently, word spreads quickly in your neighborhood. Dad and I have been answering the door all morning, and the food keeps pouring in."

"This is all from my neighbors?"

"Yep. There's more in the fridge, too."

Mom dished me up a plate of food. I ate slowly, grief still souring my appetite. But my body needed strength, and the food from my friends was infused with much-needed love and courage. So I kept up the motion, fork to mouth, chewing, swallowing, filling up my stomach.

Travis joined me at the island and kissed my cheek, and Mom served him a plate as well. Jared and Jenn, and Ben and Crystal, another brother and sister-in-law who had slept over, crept into the kitchen to hug us and whisper their condolences under the ruckus of kids running through the house laughing, playing with their cousins.

Mom said, "No one has told your kids yet, but I think you two should do it fast or they're going to hear it from someone else."

The news about their sister's death hovered like a bomb. Travis and I had no choice but to drop it, yet I balked at the devastation it would rain down on their lives. I ate my breakfast even more slowly, stretching out the minutes, soaking in their carefree laughter.

But once I'd eaten my last bite of bacon, Mom cleared my plate, then Travis's, and the galling responsibility could no longer be avoided.

Travis asked me, "How should we do this?"

It seemed like another impossible task. I didn't have an answer, so I suggested, "Let's pray before we tell them."

Travis helped me kneel beside him on our bedroom floor while he petitioned God for comfort for our children as they learned of their sister's death. The prayer strengthened us, giving our hearts a measure of peace. We called Caleb, Shaustia, and Walker into the room and sat them in a line on the edge of our bed, oldest to youngest, while we knelt in front of them.

This time it was Travis who would say the hard words. "Kids, you know that Elora was really sick when you left the hospital last night, right?"

They all nodded.

"And I know you all were praying for her to get better, but after you left, she got worse." Their eyes grew wide with worry. "It's *so* hard for us to tell you this, but in the middle of the night…our little Elora died."

I watched as each of them reacted in ways as diverse as their personalities.

Wise Caleb's face crumpled, and he fell backwards on the bed, his expression revealing that we'd confirmed his worst fear.

Faithful Shaustia had never considered that her sister might die. She gasped and threw her hands to her mouth, completely shocked, then started to cry.

Innocent Walker was too young to understand what was happening. He looked from face to face, confused, trying to learn how he should react to death.

Travis and I gathered them in a huddle on the floor and let them cry. They had so many questions.

"How did Elora die?"

"Where is she now?"

"Do we get to see her?"

"Am I going to die too?"

We soothed their heartache and fear the best we could, then we all knelt in a circle and said a family prayer, asking Heavenly Father to help us and comfort us, and to tell Elora how much we loved her and how much we would miss her.

Once the prayer was finished, Travis and I snuggled the children in our bed, wrapping them in comfort and safety for as long as they needed. One by one, they went back to their cousins and their laughter and their games. And I knew that somehow, I had to find a way to keep going. For them.

Travis and I took a few minutes of quiet for ourselves, lying still in each other's arms.

From the bedroom across the hall, Noah began to cry. Mom retrieved him almost immediately, and I could hear her in the kitchen fixing him a bottle. He fussed even as she bounced and rocked and tried to feed him.

My momma heart ached, and suddenly, I needed more than anything to be the one to do that rocking. I heaved myself out of the bed and shuffled to the living room. As soon as he saw me, Noah sat up in my mother's arms and grinned. I reached for him, and he leaned into my arms.

I held him, and cooed, and fed him his bottle, reconnecting with this patient child who had endured my unintended neglect. His tiny hand wrapped around my finger and caressed my chin, teasing smiles from me.

Without him, Elora's death would have left my arms intolerably empty.

A flash of memory lit up my mind, words from the priesthood blessing Travis had given me after I learned I couldn't have knee surgery because I was pregnant with Noah.

The baby that will be joining your family was sent at this exact time for a very specific reason. God's timing has a purpose.

I could see it. God knew this baby would be a source of comfort for me that nothing else could replace. I could hold him and feed him and bask in his innocent smiles. And he would fill me with purpose. I was his mother. He needed me.

Noah would not remember his big sister, but Elora would serve as my constant reminder to be the best mother I could be for him. For all four of them.

Four here.

One gone.

But still, all mine.

And, behold, I am with thee,
and will keep thee in all places whither thou goest,
. . . for I will not leave thee,
until I have done that which I have spoken to thee of.

GENESIS 28:15

22

FUNERAL *HOME*

ORD HAD INDEED SPREAD quickly, and as I sat on the couch in my pajamas, trying to hold myself together, family and friends opened a floodgate of support. Visitors began to arrive by mid-morning, as well as phone calls, emails, and flower deliveries.

Mom found a notebook to keep a list of the kindnesses so that one day, if I felt up to it, I could send thank-you notes. But mostly so I would never forget.

At first, the visitors were timid, afraid to intrude or overstay their welcome. But I needed people, conversation, distraction.

I wanted to talk.

To tell everyone Elora's story in my own words.

To cry and cry.

So, I asked people to stay. And they did, sitting beside me in my sorrow, helping to carry the weight of grief, then passing the responsibility on to the next group to arrive.

Mom was concerned about my strength and kept a box of Kleenex, a plate of simple finger food, and a large mug of ice water close by me at all times.

During brief lulls between visitors, Dad sat beside me, softly picking the strings of my guitar, soothing the too-quiet moments with songs from my childhood.

Kathy arrived as promised to entertain the children. She and my mom were on the phone almost as often as they weren't, making sure the whole family had heard the news of Elora's passing, but also fielding phone calls of sympathy and organizing requests for visits and meals to be brought in.

Travis preferred to keep to our bedroom, processing his grief in private, joining in visits when he felt up to it, but mostly, he wanted to be alone. And the only person he really wanted was me.

Our bedroom became a sanctuary.

When either of us needed quiet private time, we could escape there and expect not to be disturbed. Travis let me take as much time as I needed with visitors, and when he needed a quiet moment with me, I would excuse myself from the front room and be with him while our parents entertained in our stead.

Our grieving methods were polar opposite, but Travis and I gifted each other chances to mourn in the ways that helped us most.

Bishop Gast, the lay leader of our local religious congregation, asked to take on the job of finding the right funeral home to care for Elora. Travis and I were more than relieved to delegate that monumental task to a friend and religious leader we loved and trusted.

Around noon, the bishop called to let us know that Elora's body had been retrieved from the hospital that morning and was now in the care of the Warenski Funeral Home.

Mr. Warenski had asked if we could all meet that evening,

along with Bishop Gast, to begin planning Elora's funeral. It would also give us a chance to see her.

I felt woefully unprepared for both.

I asked Mom if she would come with us, to counsel us and make sure no details were overlooked. She agreed.

We didn't need to leave for over an hour, but I knew the effort to clean myself up would be laborious, and a stubborn sliver of self-respect demanded I at least make an attempt at a decent impression.

And so, I began.

The warm shower, fresh clothes, blow-dried hair, and light makeup application were equally exhausting and invigorating. By the time I stepped out of the house, I was worn out but looking decently close to my normal self, even if I didn't feel it.

Travis, Mom, and I drove into town. Bishop Gast said he'd meet us there.

I'd never been to a funeral home. Neither had Travis. The few funerals we'd attended had been held in one of our church's chapels, the same familiar places where we attended church meetings every Sunday. The only information I had about funeral homes came from Hollywood dramatizations—heavy candelabras, stained glass, organ music played in a minor key, whiffs of formaldehyde, somber, black-suited morticians with pale skin and folded hands.

The images were anything but comforting. And though she wasn't alive, I couldn't stand the thought of Elora in a place like that.

I pumped up the heater in the car and buried my hands in my coat pockets.

What's a child's funeral supposed to look like, anyway?

I had no idea. It wasn't something I'd ever expected to plan. *Who does?*

Were there rules? Expectations? Traditions?

I hoped that Mom, Bishop Gast, and the funeral director would guide us in the right direction, but they'd still expect us to make decisions about things like colors, flowers, program details, and a burial plot.

Elora deserved to have the most perfect event to celebrate her beautiful life. If not for that, I might have voted to boycott the whole thing.

I'd entirely ignored the drive of wintery gray scenery until Travis parked the van next to a house with warm-hued bricks and large bay windows. I didn't understand why we'd stopped there until I spotted an elegant sign planted in a bed of frozen flowers and frosty, spiral-trimmed evergreens. The business hours were printed on the glass of the front door, but otherwise, the Warenski Funeral Home looked just like... a home.

Mr. Warenski met the three of us in the naturally lit foyer. An arrangement of bright flowers on the entry table filled the comfortable space with fragrance. Mr. Warenski was tall and slender, with a touch of gray in his hair. He wore brown slacks, and a sport coat over his shirt and tie. His long legs crossed the plush floral rug in two steps.

"Mr. Isaacson, Mrs. Isaacson, it's nice to meet you. I'm very sorry for your loss." He shook our hands.

I introduced him to my mother, then he escorted us to his office. Other than the fact that Mr. Warenski was appropriately somber, this funeral home was nothing like I'd expected.

Bishop Gast had arrived before us, and as we entered the office, he stood to shake our hands. He wore a dark suit and tie, and had neatly slicked back his black hair.

Mr. Warenski sat in a large leather office chair behind his oak desk. "Before we begin, I want you to understand where you are."

Umm... a funeral home? A mortuary? Was there another term I'd forgotten?

He continued. "There's a reason why this building is called a funeral *home*. It's not just my place of business—it's also where my family and I live. This is our home."

Really? I hadn't expected that.

"This is where we celebrate birthdays and Christmases, where we have family dinners and read bedtime stories. This is a home that is filled with laughter and joy. This is a home where we love each other…and we have been honored to care for your little daughter Elora under this roof today."

I started to cry. It was as if he'd seen into my fears and misconceptions.

Bishop Gast was right. This was the perfect person to care for my Elora.

Mr. Warenski spent an hour helping us make simple, beautiful funeral decisions. We ordered a glossy white casket, with a spray of white and soft-pink flowers to lay over the top. The private family viewing was scheduled for Tuesday night, and the public viewing and funeral would be Wednesday morning, just four days away.

Such a short time to do so much.

Such a short time before that final goodbye.

Once everyone was satisfied that we had a good plan, Mr. Warenski asked if we would like to see Elora.

I didn't say it out loud, but I was nervous.

I'd left her body in the hospital, still warm, tucked under the blankets of her bed like she was sleeping. It was the last image I had of her. But seeing her here in the funeral home, witnessing the natural effects of death, would change that.

I knew that some people, understandably, turn away from it, choose not to witness that part of their loved one's loss. Choose to have someone else close the casket so they won't have to see.

But I couldn't.

No matter how hard it would be, there were only a few more chances for me to see my little one in this life, and I would seize every one of them.

Mr. Warenski escorted us back into the foyer while he prepared a private viewing room. Mom and I sat together on a spindle-legged settee while Travis and Bishop Gast stood nearby reviewing some of the funeral's financial details.

Mr. Warenski returned shortly, but Travis and the bishop were still deep in conversation.

Travis paused mid-sentence and turned to me. "Krista, why don't you go in first and spend a few minutes with Elora alone? I'll finish up here with Bishop Gast, then join you."

Going in alone hadn't been the plan.

I hesitated. What if being alone with Elora was more difficult than I could handle?

On the other hand, I'd been in a fish bowl ever since we arrived with Elora at the hospital. People watching me react, cry, grieve. And I'd felt an obligation to mourn in ways that everyone considered acceptable, honorable, correct.

Going in alone would give me the freedom to react however I needed to.

It sounded…safe.

But I didn't want Travis to feel left out. "You sure? I can wait if you'd rather go in together."

"No. This is good." He smiled. "You go ahead and take a few minutes alone."

I smiled back, then followed Mr. Warenski into a small, simply decorated room with two doors and no windows. One door was for us to enter from the foyer, and the other was for bringing Elora into the room.

She was there. In the center of the room laid serenely on a wheeled bed, her head gently elevated, body wrapped in a thick, warm blanket, the few remaining strands of her hair draped over her right shoulder.

I walked to her and laid my hand on the blanket over her chest, fighting against a wild surge of sorrow.

"Hi, baby girl," I whispered.

Her skin glistened, pearlescent and pale, her angelic mouth frozen in a dreamy, gentle smile. My lips quivered uncontrollably.

I looked at Mr. Warenski standing respectfully by the door. "She's beautiful. Thank you." And once I'd opened my mouth, the flood gates opened too.

Mr. Warenski retrieved a box of tissues from a small end table and held it out to me. I pulled several from the box and pressed them to my nose and mouth.

He asked, "Would you like to hold her?"

"Yes," I said between convulsive sobs.

He gestured to an upholstered armchair. "If you sit here, I'll bring her to you."

I sat as Mr. Warenski gathered the blanket tightly around Elora. He gently lifted her and placed her in my lap. Her skin was cold, but the blanket provided me with the comforting illusion of cradling her warmly.

Mr. Warenski left through the door to the foyer, and it was just me and my girl.

I spent thirty sacred minutes alone with Elora.

I sang to her, and rocked her, and memorized every detail of her face—her long, dark eyelashes, the blister on her upper lip from sucking her fingers, the placement of the dimple in her cheek, the shape of her nose—everything. I even caressed the ugly, jagged, stapled scar covering the left side of her shaved scalp, wishing fiercely I could have saved her from that pain.

I cried unrestrained, told her all of the private feelings in my heart, and made her solemn promises.

Her spirit was near. I felt sure that she heard me. It may even have been her spirit hands that wrapped around my heart, holding the shattered pieces together.

When Travis joined me, we spent a few minutes together with Elora, but I wanted him to have the same experience alone with her that I had enjoyed, so I made him sit. I passed Elora into his arms and left.

Bishop Gast had gone home, so I sat with Mom on the settee and chattered away about plans for the funeral as a distraction to keep myself from publicly breaking down.

Mr. Warenski checked on Travis after thirty minutes. He returned with a message that Travis wanted Mom and me to join him.

Elora was back on the bed. Travis and I stood off to the side to let Mom approach her alone. She cried, and touched Elora's hands. We let her take the time she needed, then all agreed it was time to go.

I lightly kissed Elora's cheek, knowing we would be back in a few days to dress and prepare her for the funeral.

I still wished more than anything that I could lift her from the bed and carry her home. But I resigned myself to the relief of knowing that she would be well cared for here, in this funeral *home*.

. . . I do know that whosoever shall put their trust in God
shall be supported in their trials,
and their troubles, and their afflictions,
and shall be lifted up at the last day.

ALMA 36:3

23

PAY IT FORWARD

BACK IN THE CAR, Travis steered the van out of the parking lot in the direction of home, but Mom had an idea.

"Krista, how are you feeling?"

"I'm all right, Mom. I'm glad that part is over."

"Well, I was thinking that since we're already out, and if you still have a bit of energy, we could do some shopping. Get started on the things we need for the funeral."

It was a good idea. There was so little time to get everything done.

Travis answered, "That's fine with me. As long as you ladies let me buy you dinner first."

We settled on a fast-casual Chinese restaurant where we wouldn't have to talk to a waiter. I chose a table by the window where the evening sun streaming through the glass fell deliciously warm on my arms and face.

The people around us went about their evening, unaware of the trauma we'd just experienced. Anonymity felt strangely peaceful. I didn't have to talk, or explain, or cry. I could just sit, eat my crispy orange chicken with fried rice, and be quiet.

Travis reached across the table and held my hand while Mom smiled and chatted, and for a moment, I felt like me.

The food, rest, and normalcy gave me a small boost of energy and courage as we walked into Walmart. But while the store was the same as it always had been, I wasn't. The crowds, noise, and endless rows of colorful items quickly overwhelmed me, and I wasn't sure how long I'd last.

Travis took off on his own to look for matching funeral neckties for him, Caleb, and Walker.

Mom insisted I push a shopping cart—something to lean on, to balance my unsteady legs, and reserve my strength. I set a slow but steady pace as we walked toward the clothing department.

"Honey," Mom said, "have you thought about what you're going to wear? Do you want to look for a new dress?"

I considered it briefly, but decided a new dress would be a waste of money. I'd never wear it again. It would always represent the day I buried my daughter, and I couldn't imagine ever wanting to drape myself in it again.

"I'll just find something in my closet," I answered. I was sure I had something that would work, an outfit with pleasant memories already infused into the fabric.

So, instead of stopping in the women's department, we headed to the little girls' section. We rounded a corner and suddenly, I was surrounded by racks of darling things Elora would have loved.

The ache in my chest deepened—agony at the realization that once we had everything for her funeral, I would never have an occasion to buy things for Elora again. No more Christmases or birthdays.

Her third birthday was only six weeks away. I'd already bought her a new doll and hidden it in my closet. And we were supposed to go on a mommy/daughter date to pick out a new Sunday dress.

Now, I would have to pick it for her. Only I didn't want to.

I had decided at the funeral home to clothe Elora in angelic white.

I'd dressed her in white before, on the day of her baby blessing. Her blessing gown was long and lacy, with puffed sleeves. I'd made a tiny corsage from white ribbons, lace, and miniature roses and tied it around her newborn wrist.

Travis had held her in front of our church congregation, surrounded by a circle of her grandpas and uncles, and spoken a blessing from God just for her.

That little white corsage was safely stored with her gown, wrapped in tissue paper, in my cedar chest. My plan was for Elora to wear the corsage again on two future white-dress days.

When she turned eight years old, I would buy her second white dress and she would wear the little corsage in her hair for her baptism day.

And then, one day she would announce she was getting married. We would buy her third white dress, the most beautiful of all, and I would pin the corsage to a white handkerchief for her to carry during the wedding ceremony.

I had never planned on *this* white dress.

I stood in the aisle, leaning on the cart, while Mom wandered through the racks. She easily found a white slip, white tights, and white ballet slippers, but there was not a white dress to be found.

"Why don't we try a dress shop?" Mom suggested.

But I couldn't bear it.

It was one thing to stand in the middle of Walmart with crowds of people who looked past me and didn't ask questions. Quite another to go to a small dress shop and explain that I was there to choose a dress for my daughter's funeral.

It was too soon. My strength was spent, my heart, broken, and I just couldn't face it.

I leaned heavily on the bar of the shopping cart, weary in every way, tears threatening. "Mom, I just want to go home."

She didn't argue.

We found Travis and made our few purchases, then the three of us walked slowly to the car. I closed my eyes while Travis drove and tried to ignore the nagging thought that Elora's dress would still need to be bought. And soon.

Back at home, I changed into pajamas and hid in my closet to think about white dresses and cry. Tomorrow was Sunday, a holy day that I chose to keep free from activities like shopping, which meant I had until Monday to work up the courage to go out and try again. But even thinking about the effort it would take filled me with despair.

I knelt on the floor of my darkened closet and prayed.

Father, I don't know how to do this. I want to buy Elora a beautiful dress, but I don't know how to find it or choose it. It hurts so much, and I'm so tired. I'm going to try again on Monday. Will you help me know where to look so I can find the right dress quickly and easily?

I finished my prayer, but stayed in the closet to cry a bit more.

Buzz.

My cell phone lit up.

I glanced at the name on the screen, expecting to ignore the call until I saw that it was Melanie.

Travis's cousin Rob and his wife, Melanie, had lost a baby son only eighteen months previously. If anyone could understand my heart, it was Melanie.

I answered the phone—croaky voice, runny nose, and all.

"Melanie, I'm so glad it's you."

"Oh, Krista, my heart has been with you all day. How are you?"

"We just got back from the funeral home. I got to hold her."

"How was it?"

"Really hard and really…sacred."

"Yeah. I remember."

I knew she did. That holding her son's body was seared into her memory the same way holding Elora would forever be seared into mine.

"Melanie, how did you get through it?"

"The same way you will. With lots of love and support from God and from all of the people around you. Which is actually why I'm calling."

I wiped my nose on my sleeve. "Okay…" I shifted into a more comfortable position on the floor.

"I have a neighbor named Marianne. You've never met her. Marianne lost a daughter a couple years ago in a car accident."

"Oh, Melanie, I hate hearing that."

"Yeah. Marianne was devastated. It was so sudden."

I'd had thirty precious hours with Elora to process her illness, her death, to say goodbye. What would it be like not to have that chance? That time? To have someone you love just… gone?

My heart ached for this mama I'd never met.

Melanie continued, "Marianne's an amazing seamstress, and the thing she wanted most was to sew her daughter a burial dress. But she couldn't do it. It was too hard on her."

Oh, how well I understood. I started to cry again, but breathed slowly through the tears so Melanie wouldn't hear.

"But then, a woman Marianne had never met, a seamstress, heard her story and volunteered to sew the dress. It was a miracle for Marianne, and she decided that someday she would pay that miracle forward."

My heart thumped hard in my chest.

"Krista, I was telling Marianne about Elora, and she asked me to find out if you already have a dress for her to be buried in."

"Melanie, you can't really be asking me this."

"Why not?"

"Because I'm literally talking to you from the floor of my closet where I've been crying and praying that somehow I'd have the courage to go shopping Monday to pick one out. I honestly didn't know how I was going to do it."

"Well, how about you don't worry anymore. Marianne wants to sew the dress, if you'll let her."

Tears dripped from my chin. "I would love that."

With Melanie's help, I decided on a white satin ankle-length dress with simple trim.

Size 3T.

I offered to buy the fabric, but Melanie wouldn't hear of it.

"This is a gift from me and Marianne. One that's being paid forward, and now it's in your court. Take it, and do something special with it."

I'd never be a seamstress. My sewing machine and I didn't get along very well. I wouldn't be a link in the chain of white-dress makers. But that didn't matter. I was sure if I kept my eyes and heart open, someday God would show me how to use my own talents to pay Marianne's kindness forward.

"Melanie, tell Marianne I'll find a way. I promise."

*... He that endureth in faith
and doeth my will,
the same shall overcome...*

DOCTRINE AND COVENANTS 63:20

24

FEVERISH

I HURRIED FROM MY CLOSET into the living room to share the miraculous news of Elora's dress with the family members visiting there. With my heart temporarily lightened by the removal of that burden, I eagerly joined in their conversation, but the longer I sat, the heavier the grief and exhaustion of the day weighed on me.

I still hadn't slept an entire night through, and the hours of steadily pushing against the flood of sorrow had resulted in a massive headache. I was torn between the need for people to talk to and the need for rest. But as the night sky darkened, the visitors, emails, and phone calls naturally tapered off. The room grew quiet, thick with the inescapable pain of missing Elora.

Travis stepped outside to clear his head in the brisk winter air, but before he'd closed the door, he called inside to me.

"Babe. Come here. You need to see this."

I joined Travis on the porch. Someone had lined the driveway with brightly lit luminaries decorated with handwritten words like "Faith," "Hope," "Family," and "Love."

We went back into the house and helped our kids put on their shoes and coats, then we all went outside together and walked the driveway. Mom and Dad stood in the doorway while my little family huddled together on the lawn, skin glowing in gifted luminary light, hoping that heaven's newest little angel was joining us in that family hug.

Mom put the kids to bed after I'd hugged them a little longer than usual. Travis followed not long after. But even as my body begged for sleep, I was afraid to try. Taking a nap earlier in the day had been safer with everyone else awake to keep the house full of chatter and distraction. I feared the quiet, dark hours alone without other people's voices to drive away the monsters in my head. So, I ignored the throbbing behind my eyes and stayed up for as long as my parents would keep talking.

Mom brought me two ibuprofen and a fresh glass of water. Surviving my first day without Elora had been like fighting quicksand. The mire of my grief sucking at my legs.

Engulfing.

Swallowing.

Dragging on me. Constantly.

Every visitor, every gift delivered, each evidence of God's love had been a branch thrust out to my rescue, something to grasp on to, to keep my head above the surface. But now that the house was quiet and all distractions missing, would those branches be enough to hold me until morning? Or would the grief slowly creep up and consume me? I was petrified to find out.

The luminary lights continued to glow encouragingly through the glass panel of the front door. I traced the pattern of the door's wood grain with my eyes. I'd once come through that doorway holding brand-new baby Elora in my arms. Bringing her home for the first time. Only joy in my heart. No idea how little time I'd have with her.

Everything reminded me of her—every corner of the house, every object held a memory. Her smile haunted me from pictures on the walls. Every space echoed with her absence. My yearning to hold her, to kiss her, gnawed at me relentlessly.

I broke down, and Mom wrapped her arms around me.

"Mom, it hurts so bad! I don't know how I'm going to do this. Every day. For the rest of my life."

She listened and cried with me, held me until that surge of agony had subsided.

Eventually, Mom and Dad both admitted they couldn't stay awake a minute longer. Mom walked me to my bedroom door. "Try to sleep, sweetheart. Every day will get a tiny bit easier."

I wanted that to be true, but I'd barely made it through one day. How would I endure weeks, months, years of longing for my girl?

I had to stop thinking about it that way. About forever. Stop trying to survive ahead of right now. "I'll try," I told her.

"And don't worry if you hear the baby cry. I'll get up with him tonight. You just sleep."

"Thanks, Mom. For everything. I don't know what I would have done today if you hadn't come."

"You couldn't have kept me away." She hugged me, then waited until I closed the door behind me.

Travis snored softly, so I kept the bedroom light off and changed into my pajamas in the dark. Elora's sunflower pj's lay folded on my nightstand, but I didn't want to disturb Travis by laying them out between us again. I touched a kiss to my fingertips, brushed them over the fabric, then tried not to shake the mattress as I slipped beneath the covers.

Elora filled my mind and wandered the darkened hallways

of my home, reminding me of all the last places she'd touched. I wandered with her, mopping at my tears with my bedsheet.

I cried in silence for a long time before sleep finally crept over me. But it didn't help. Haunted, indecipherable dreams kept my rest shallow and fitful. And when the ibuprofen I'd taken before bed wore off in the middle of the night, my headache returned, accompanied by an achy fever. I woke Travis and asked him to bring more medicine. He helped me sit up so I could swallow the pills he'd brought, then I let my head fall back heavily onto my sickly warm pillow. My eyes stung, but closing my eyelids only lit them on fire.

Travis crawled over me to his side of the bed. "Is there anything else I can get you?"

"No. I just think everything's finally catching up with me."

"I know. But I'm right here. Don't hesitate to wake me again."

"I won't."

His soft snore picked up a short time later. I matched the rhythm of his breathing to my own until my aching body finally suppressed my mind and I slept deeply. Four hours later, I woke drenched in sweat, shaking with chills.

Travis was already awake, the muffled timbre of his voice drifting from the kitchen through my bedroom wall. I rolled onto my side and attempted to prop myself up on one elbow so I could call for him, but a sharp pain under that arm stole my breath and collapsed my body back onto the mattress.

What was that?

I gently used my other hand to prod under my arm. The skin was hot to the touch and very tender around a lump of hard tissue near the edge of my breast.

Mastitis, maybe? An infection common in breastfeeding

mothers. *Especially in mothers who've had to stop feeding their babies cold turkey,* I thought with sadness.

My symptoms all pointed to it. The headache, the fever, the pain and warmth under my arm.

And the best way to fight it? An antibiotic. Which would mean a trip to the doctor.

But it's Sunday. Everyone's closed.

Except the ER.

The last place in the world I wanted to visit was the emergency room of the hospital. It was too soon.

"Trav?" I called his name three times before he heard.

He sat on the edge of the bed and pressed the back of his hand to my forehead. "How're you feeling? Any better?"

"No. Worse."

He winced and shook his hand. "Ooh. You're burning up!"

"I think I might have an infection." I described my symptoms. "And I think I need to see a doctor, but I'm begging you not to take me back to the emergency room. I don't think I could handle it."

He moved to the rocking chair by the bed and opened his laptop. He found an Instacare clinic reasonably close by that was open on weekends. I agreed to go there.

Mom helped me dress, and I leaned on Travis as he helped me to the car. The ibuprofen hadn't touched my fever, and my skin ached under the slightest pressure. Luckily, there was no one else in line when we reached the clinic, and I was shown right into an exam room.

The disposable paper crinkled as I climbed onto the table rehearsing how I would explain to the doctor that I hadn't been able to nurse my baby because Elora was sick and then she died.

I still didn't like saying it out loud. Especially to strangers. What a way to begin a conversation. "Hello, my name is Krista, and one interesting fact about me is... well, my daughter died yesterday." No matter how I practiced it in my head, it was a horrible thing to have to throw out there. But the doctor came before I'd finished rehearsing and asked why I was there, and somehow the words tumbled out.

He examined me and confirmed that a mastitis infection was the culprit. With great sympathy, he offered to speed up my healing with an antibiotic shot, which I agreed to readily. Before I left his office, he handed me a list of additional home remedies —warm compresses, ibuprofen, and a breast pump. "The pump is your best option. It will really speed up your recovery. Do you have one?"

"No," I said.

"I'd recommend that you buy or borrow one. Today, if possible."

Travis helped me into the car, then backed out and headed across the parking lot toward the same Walmart we'd left only hours before.

"Trav, I can't. I don't want to go in there."

"But babe, the doctor thinks a pump will really help you."

"I know, but I can't move. I hurt too much."

"All the more reason we should try everything we can."

"It's just..." The truth was hard to speak. It seemed ridiculous, and yet, to me, it wasn't. "There will be all those people in there. Like last night. And they'll be shopping and doing normal things. And I'll have to smile and pretend that nothing horrible just happened to me, and I'll have to talk to people. And..." I thought about how hard the shopping trip yesterday had been.

I hurt all over, inside and out, and I longed for the safety of my home, felt desperate to get back to it. "Can we just go home?"

"Why don't I go in by myself?" The lines of stress and exhaustion on his face told me he was as worn out as I was.

"I know you would do that for me, but I have no idea what options there are or how to tell you what I need. And I really don't want you to leave me. Can we just go home? Please."

"Okay. I only want you to feel better as fast as possible."

"I know. I think if I rest today, I'll start to feel a little better and then Mom and I can try to go to the store tomorrow. Or I'm sure I can borrow a pump from a friend. I'll figure something out. I just can't do it right now."

Travis didn't argue me down further. Without another word, he turned the car around, toward the road and home.

I will not leave you comfortless:
I will come to you.

JOHN 14:18

25

ENVELOPED

$\mathcal{T}$RAVIS HELPED ME back to bed. Exhausted by the visit to the doctor and relieved to be back home, I fell asleep almost instantly and slept for a couple of hours until someone sat on the edge of my bed and rubbed my arm. When I opened my eyes, Mom was holding the phone out toward me.

"Your friend Heidi is on the phone, and I think you'll want to talk to her."

Heidi. My friend who comforted me in the lobby of the hospital just as I was headed upstairs to tell the doctor to take Elora off life support. I'd told Heidi what I was about to do and then left her standing there. I sat up gingerly and took the phone from my mom.

"Heidi? Hey, my friend." My voice was rough and groggy, but I knew Heidi wouldn't care.

"Krista... I can't even tell you how sorry I am."

"Thank you. It's hard. I'm missing her pretty badly today."

"I can't imagine."

"Heidi, I'm so sorry I left you in the hospital lobby like that. I wasn't really in my right mind."

"Are you kidding me? That's the last thing you need to worry about."

"Okay." Good. I hadn't permanently scarred my friend.

"Krista, ever since seeing you at the hospital yesterday, I haven't stopped thinking about you. You remember I'm a lactation specialist, right?"

"Um, yeah. I remember."

"Well, I know you have a new baby, and I can't shake the feeling that you need a breast pump. I have a brand-new one sitting right here, and if you want, I'd love to bring it over to you."

"Are you serious?" The tears made my head hurt even worse, but I couldn't stop them.

"Yes," Heidi said. "I'm serious."

Mom cried quietly beside me, listening while I told Heidi about my illness, my trip to the doctor, and my inability to face the store. "This is a literal answer to my prayers."

Within the hour, Heidi had dropped off the pump and showed me how to use it. When she left, I slept for a couple more hours, then woke up feeling like it had already begun to make a difference.

Eventually my hunger grew fiercer than my fever, so I crawled out of bed and walked very slowly to the kitchen, my right hand brushing the wall to steady myself.

Travis sat with several family members from his side and mine around the kitchen table. They scolded me for being up and pressed me to return to bed, but I convinced them that for now, their company would be better medicine than more sleep.

They took turns filling me in on the phone calls, emails, and visitors I'd missed, and the messages of love people had asked each of them to relay. Amazing meals had continued to be delivered with so much food that we'd started to run out of room to store the leftovers in the fridge. The number of people reaching out to support us had grown to such astounding numbers that Mom kept her list of kindnesses near her at all times. She displayed the gifts and flowers on every available surface in the living room, found a basket for the growing stack of cards, and kept a pad of paper near the phone to jot down personal messages relayed verbally.

The love of my family and friends surged through me, granting me momentary respite as vital and life-sustaining as oxygen.

The kitchen counter was spread with a smorgasbord, and knowing I would want to sample every dish that my friends had delivered, Travis put a bite of everything on a plate for me.

I nearly had a spoonful of frog's eye pasta salad to my mouth when a little nephew toddled past me carrying Elora's favorite stuffed duck. I'd bought it before she was born and packed it in my hospital bag along with a tiny pink nightgown and crocheted baby blanket. After the nurses gave Elora her first bath and wheeled her into my room, I'd laid that duckie next to her in the bassinet, her very first gift, and Travis and I had laughed because it was nearly bigger than she was.

I set down my spoon.

No one at the table questioned me as I left my plate of food untouched and walked into Elora's bedroom. No one noticed me bribe my little nephew into trading the duck for a bear. But after fifteen minutes, when I didn't come back, Travis came looking for me.

He found me kneeling on the floor of our bedroom, my arms full of Elora's special things, arranging them in a pile by my side of the bed. Her favorite stuffed animals, dolls, and blankets.

Her plastic princess shoes and tiara. The plastic bag of toys and crayons she'd received in the hospital and carried around every day since her tonsillectomy. Her red hooded sweater. Her pink piggy purse with three quarters from Grandma, two peanuts in their shells, and one marble still safely stowed inside. Her Winnie the Pooh shoes, coloring book, flower headbands we'd bought to hide her buzzed hair, and the green-striped t-shirt from the hospital.

Everything I didn't want anyone else to touch. No one else's fingerprints to replace Elora's.

Travis knelt beside me and rubbed my back. "You okay?"

"Mmhmm." I finished my arrangement, ensuring that every item was visible and none of the dolls' faces were smothered.

We sat quietly in front of the little shrine until I was ready to return to the family. Travis helped me back to the kitchen, and I finished my plate of food.

In the early afternoon, after our regular Sunday church services had ended, Bishop Gast called. Understandably, our family had been absent from worship service that day, but he also knew that our absence meant we'd missed the weekly Sabbath tradition of the sacrament—an ordinance where members of our faith eat bread and drink water that has been blessed in remembrance of Christ and His atoning sacrifice. A sacred source of peace and strength.

I could hear the bishop's voice through the phone receiver as he spoke with Travis. "I figured if ever there was a time your family could use the power and comfort of the sacrament, it's now."

He had asked two young men who were authorized to prepare and bless the sacrament to accompany him to our home.

We were touched by his thoughtfulness, and despite my illness, we agreed to their visit.

Bishop Gast and the young men arrived dressed in their Sunday best. My parents, Travis, our children, and I sat around the coffee table in our front room while the young men laid out the sacrament trays, one with bite-sized pieces of bread, another filled with tiny paper cups of water. They covered the trays with a white cloth, then recited the familiar prayers I'd heard thousands of times.

"O God, the Eternal Father, we ask thee in the name of thy Son, Jesus Christ, to bless and sanctify this bread to the souls of all those who partake of it; that they may eat in remembrance of the body of thy Son, and witness unto thee, O God, the Eternal Father, that they are willing to take upon them the name of thy Son, and always remember him, and keep his commandments which he hath given them, that they may always have his Spirit to be with them" (Moroni 4:3).

Nearly every Sunday of my life, I'd partaken of the bread and water that symbolized this promise—that as long as I remembered my Savior, He would always be with me. But not until that moment, listening to the words of the prayer through the lens of loss and trauma, did I truly *hear* the promise and understand it. While Elora was in the hospital and every second since, I'd been abundantly witnessing the fulfillment of Christ's promise to be with me.

The young men passed the tray of bread to my family, then the tray of water. My body still ached with fever, and my heart with mourning, but as I ate and drank those sacred emblems of Jesus' sacrifice and thought of the myriad ways He had kept His promise to me, the Holy Spirit entered the room, warm, and bright, and loving. Seeping into the walls, ceilings, and floors. Soaking into the furniture, carpets, and drapes. And most importantly, radiating into my family's hearts and minds and souls until even the air in our home felt cleansed and holy.

I hadn't fully noticed until that moment how the love and service poured out by friends and family, all of the merciful blessings from God, the attention of angels, and Jesus' gentle care had been transforming our home into a sacred space. A place of healing and comfort. Where God's blessings sustained us, wrapped us in safety, and held us together while we began the agonizing process of learning to live without Elora. Our family, our home, was being enveloped in God's love and Christ's mercy. Like a bubble.

It was why I'd begged to return home after shopping at Walmart, and again after the doctor's office. And why so many visitors commented about the special feeling that had enveloped them as they crossed our threshold.

I didn't know how long it would last, only that my family needed it as much as air or food, and that I would do whatever it took to keep it around us for as long as possible.

26

HANDS

THE REMAINDER of the Sabbath was truly a welcome day of rest. I napped until early evening, then took my time getting out of bed. Mom was in the kitchen re-heating a gifted dinner, Dad was downstairs playing with the kids, and Travis was on his laptop in the living room. I curled up next to him on the couch.

"How are you feeling, sweetheart?" he asked.

"I still ache all over, but I slept a little better."

"That's good." He adjusted the blanket in his lap and spread an edge over my legs.

"What are you working on?" I asked.

"I had a few ideas for Elora's obituary that I wanted to write down before I forgot them."

"Really? Show me."

Travis turned the screen toward me, and I read aloud.

"'Elora was an angel to us with her smiles, and snuggles, and her love and laughter. Her parents, big sister, and three brothers will miss her dearly. She will be with them always. They look forward to holding her again in a place much brighter and more glorious—a place more like their little Elora.'"

A mixture of adoration and ache gushed from my heart. How had Travis managed to keep his composure and find the words to give Elora such a tender tribute? Every time I'd tried to think about it, I'd risked unleashing an emotional tsunami. It was all I could do to keep my turbulent emotions from exploding through the gaping wound of my grief.

Talking to visitors gave my anguish a place to overflow, a measured, messy leak that relieved enough pressure to prevent a cataclysmic meltdown. But to attempt to condense Elora's life, her personality, and my intense love for her into a single paragraph?

I couldn't.

I leaned my head against Travis's arm while tears ran down my fevered cheeks. "I don't know how you did that. Every time I've thought about what I'd want to say in her obituary, it hurts so badly, I have to stop and think about something else."

"And I couldn't *stop* thinking about it. I want people to know how precious she is, that we'll always miss her, but also that we know where she is and we'll get to see her again."

"It's beautiful. Words of love from her daddy. I'm sure she loves it."

Mom brought two plates of warm lasagna, French bread, and Caesar salad to us on the couch—mine with a side of ibuprofen. She served the kids their meal in the kitchen, then she and Dad brought their plates into the living room and joined us.

"Oh, my word, honey," Mom said to me between mouthfuls of noodles. "You can't believe the phone calls I've been getting while you were asleep."

"From who?" I said, taking a small bite of bread.

"Well, besides all of the people calling to check on you or wanting to contribute to the funeral in some way, people have been calling to say that they're coming for the funeral, that they're on their way to you right now, or planning to be in the next day or two. It's like the whole world is on the move."

I set my slice of bread on my plate. "Who, Mom? Who's coming?"

Mom reported name after name of family members who were so set on supporting us, they wouldn't be daunted by the harsh winter weather.

An aunt and uncle were cutting short an overseas vacation and would be on the first available flight home.

Family members from both mine and Travis's sides were traveling from California, Arizona, Washington, and Southern Utah.

My elderly Grandma Walker was catching a ride from the Boise area with a caravan of aunts, uncles, and cousins, as well as my sister Rachel and her husband, Clark.

Two of my brothers had recently traveled to different states to start new sales jobs—Brian to Arizona, Lance to Georgia. They had both spent much of the money they'd earned to buy plane tickets and get to me as fast as they could.

My college student sister, Alicia, had bought a Greyhound ticket and would brave traveling alone from Rexburg, Idaho, on a crowded bus the next morning.

My brother Michael and sister-in-law Deanna had packed their four kids into their SUV and set off from Omaha hoping to beat a blizzard, but instead drove straight into it. They had white-knuckle-gripped through hundreds of miles of white-out conditions. In Wyoming, it got so bad they stopped at a big-box store, bought a good set of snow tire chains, a shovel, and an emergency heater, and after several prayers, kept driving.

"I've been so anxious about every one of them," Mom confessed, "but I haven't stopped praying for them. And if the blessings continue, people will start to arrive tomorrow."

My appetite dissolved into amazement, and I set my dinner plate on the coffee table.

All of those people. They were coming. Loved ones on the move toward me, drawing closer every minute. Strengthening the ranks of hands, both mortal and angelic, that had already been holding me steady since the hospital.

Hands.

A memory stirred from my college days, a team-building game where I'd stood in the center of a tight circle of my classmates who were seated on the floor, their hands outstretched like a wall surrounding me. On the count of three, I was instructed to fall. In any direction. Just close my eyes, stay stiff like a board, and fall. It had taken a minute to steel my courage, but eventually I'd crossed my arms over my chest and let my body lean hard to the left, logic blaring that I was about to hit the floor.

But I didn't.

The wall of hands caught me, and as they pushed me back toward the center, other hands caught me. Passing me around and around until my confidence in them was sure. It didn't matter which way I leaned—they never once let me fall.

"How is this happening?" I blurted after Mom finished listing people.

Dad punched an emphatic fork of lasagna into the air. "Because that's what you do when you care about someone. You go."

Mom saluted him with her water glass. "Amen."

God was sending reinforcements. People I trusted and loved in whom my confidence was already solid. And no matter how hard the grief pressed over the next three days, all of those hands would surround me, hold me up, and ensure that I would never hit the ground.

Be merciful unto me, O God,
be merciful unto me: for my soul trusteth in thee:
yea, in the shadow of thy wings will I make my refuge,
until these calamities be overpast.

PSALM 57:1

27

TREES

By Monday morning, the antibiotic shot had started to kick in, and my fever was significantly lower, though not gone. More than anything, I wanted to ignore reality, stay in bed, and try to sleep away the pain, but there was too much to do. So, despite my dread and exhaustion and feverish body, I forced myself out of bed and into the shower.

The most urgent task for the day was to choose a cemetery and buy Elora's burial plot. Her "final resting place."

I disliked that description. It suggested we'd simply gone on a long walk and found a lovely spot to rest for a picnic lunch. It wasn't a *resting* place. It was a *burial* place, as in *under* the ground where I'd never see her, or hear her, or touch her again for the rest of my life. I wouldn't actually witness that moment. It would happen after our family had left the cemetery, after we had returned to the church to be served a lovely homemade meal. That's when Elora would be lowered into the ground.

Into the dark, the cold.

Alone.

And even if I wasn't there to see it, I would know. I would feel it.

Because a piece of my heart would go with her. It had already broken to shards, so I had reserved a fragment to be buried in the place where she lay. So she would know I was with her. So she wouldn't be scared.

And now it was up to us to choose that place for her. Only I didn't know how. How could I put my beautiful child in the ground, cover her with mounds of earth, and leave her there?

Taking Elora's body to the cemetery was the hardest thing left on the list for me to do.

I finished getting ready, but before I left my room, I knelt beside my bed. "Heavenly Father, today is going to be hard, and this is probably the millionth time I've asked, but I need your help. And please give Elora a hug from me. Tell her I miss her every second."

I stayed on my knees until my first cry of the day had worn itself out. Then I helped Caleb, Shaustia, and Walker get breakfast, fed baby Noah, and doled out extra helpings of hugs and kisses to each of them.

Mom and Dad volunteered to stay home and watch the kids so Travis and I could have some alone time to visit cemeteries. A gift of a few hours to reconnect with each other, but also, of privacy. To nurture each other through the unique parental responsibility of choosing a burial spot for our child.

I slipped on my shoes, took my coat and purse from their hook in the mud room, and nearly told Travis I was ready to go, but a little voice called from the bathroom. "Mommy? Ca' you holp me?"

Walker had attempted to squeeze toothpaste onto his Batman toothbrush by himself, resulting in a gooey, bubblegum-scented mess he didn't know how to fix. I jumped at the chance to be useful to him. Together we wiped the blue goo from the counter and rinsed his brush, then I loaded it with just the right amount of toothpaste and held him up to the sink. He scrubbed until the toothpaste foamed, then gave me a bubbly smile in the mirror.

He needs me.

And that simple reminder gave me courage.

I kissed Walker's foamy cheek and sputtered in pretend shock at the bubbles on my lips. He giggled. I rinsed both our faces, dried him with a towel, and watched him run downstairs to play.

Courage.

I walked outside to the car and held Travis's hand as we drove away.

The two cemeteries closest to our home lie in the same direction, so that's the way we headed. We were quiet at first, holding hands, soaking in the comfort of each other. But the first cemetery was only a short drive away, and we needed to begin our decision.

"Trav?" I said. "Have you thought about what it should look like? The plot, I mean. Is there anything you want?"

"I don't know. I guess I hope I'll just know it when I see it."

"Yeah. Me too." But now I was thinking. "It should be beautiful, though, right? And quiet?"

"Yes," Travis said, which started him thinking too. "With a really nice view. Maybe of the mountains." Whether skiing, mountain biking, camping, or hiking, Travis's soul always sought peace in the mountains.

"And it has to have trees. Big ones," I added.

Trees were important. They were the closest thing I could think of to the shelter of my own arms. Elora needed big trees to keep her safe.

The closest cemetery was new with lots of plots available, but the trees were still saplings held steady by wooden stakes driven into the ground. On the other hand, American Fork Cemetery, twenty minutes away, was old, and the giant sycamores had been planted generations ago. American Fork also offered the possibility of a beautiful mountain view.

So, it was decided. We drove past the closer cemetery toward American Fork.

Travis circled the cemetery, past a flagpole and a war memorial, until we spotted a short, bricked office building with a backhoe parked at the far end.

He steered the car directly in front of the glass doors, but didn't turn off the ignition, which wasn't like him. He hated the waste of an idling engine.

I squeezed his hand. "I'm not ready either."

We sat together breathing for a couple of minutes, and when he finally released my hand and opened his door, I followed.

As we stepped into the office, it dawned on me that for once we wouldn't have to explain our situation. For once it would be obvious why we were there.

"Hello," Travis said to the lady seated behind the desk. "We need to buy a burial plot."

The cemetery administrator asked us questions about what type of plot we wanted, then circled five available spots on a map of the cemetery and chauffeured us in a golf cart to view them. The icy wind cut at the skin on my face, so I zipped the neck of my coat up over my mouth and nose to reduce the sting. The wind was coldest on clear days, but at least the ground was free of snow. We'd get a good look at each spot.

The first plot was too close to the noisy city road. The second was in a newer corner where the trees had not yet grown tall. But when I stepped out of the golf cart to inspect plot number three, it was like Travis had said. I just knew this was the one.

The plot was at the edge of a lawn and framed in by an historic rock wall of quartzite, sandstone, and marble. Many of the surrounding headstones were ancient and crumbling, marked with the insignia of war heroes or historic pioneer heritage. In the spring, the sprawling, winter-barren limbs of a nearby sycamore would grow thick with leaves, shielding Elora from the summer sun. And in the fall, they would cover her in a thick, warm blanket of blazing orange, my favorite color. But for now, while the world was frozen and brown, the majestic, snow-capped Mt. Timpanogos to the east would stand sentinel over Elora's spot and guard her through the winter.

I nodded to Travis, and he nodded back. "We don't need to see any more," I said to the administrator. "This is the one."

The administrator carted us back to the office, but by the time we walked through the glass doors, I was second-guessing our choice. Plot number three was just as picturesque as I'd hoped, and the trees were exactly what I'd wanted, but no place would ever be lovely enough to overpower the sorrow of its purpose.

But I had no choice. No amount of wishing or fighting would allow Elora to come home.

I whispered another prayer for strength. *Father, help me.*

We purchased the plot and signed the necessary paperwork in permanent black ink. I recapped the pen and slid the paper back across the desk.

On our way out of the cemetery, we drove past the plot one more time, just to be sure, but my heart was no longer trustworthy.

Heavenly Father, did we pick the right spot? I want Elora to have a beautiful place where our family can visit her and find peace. Tell me that someday it will be.

But if He answered me, His words were lost to my fixation on a piece of land that would soon be scarred with a child-sized hole. All I could hear was the creaking and snapping of bone-bare sycamore branches.

We didn't go home. Neither of us was ready. We needed time together to think, to process, to love away a tiny bit of the hurt.

Travis drove aimlessly through town. Up one street. Back down another. West, then east. Turning when he felt like it. But no matter how much distance we put between us and the cemetery, I couldn't leave it behind.

I stroked the back of Travis's hand with my thumb. There wasn't anyone alive who could fully understand what Elora's loss was doing to my heart except him.

Since the early days of our marriage, whenever I had a rough day, Travis would pretend to be an aloe plant. He'd snap both of his hands forward at the wrists, like snapping off the end of an aloe branch, then pretend to rub the soothing balm all over me until I couldn't hold back the laughter. No matter how bad things got, he'd always been my best medicine. And even driving in silence beside him was a balm.

Eventually, we passed between the stone pillars that marked the entrance to our neighborhood. I sighed. Part of me wanted to keep driving forever. Another part of me really wanted to hug and kiss my kids. But all of me wanted a nap.

When my red front door came into view, something unusual caught my eye.

Soft white light illuminated the normally shaded front porch. Travis let me out in the driveway to investigate.

Hidden behind the porch pillar stood a silk tree potted in a dark bronze planter. The glossy leaves were strung with translucent red heart beads, white heart-shaped lights, and hung with dozens of pictures of Jesus and handwritten notes of love and support. I lifted the tree by the pot and carried it into the front room, re-plugging in the lights by the front door.

Travis came in from the garage. "Wow! Who's that from?"

"I don't know yet. But there are tons of notes all over it."

Travis and I circled the tree, admiring the pictures and reading every note until we pieced together that it had been decorated by a girls' youth group in our neighborhood and their leaders.

"Where should we put it?" Travis asked.

I knew the perfect spot and carried the tree to our bedroom, plugging it in so the light cascaded over the bed. The glow lit the pictures of Jesus' face.

Travis watched from the doorway.

"Will that bother you, honey?" I asked him.

"Just the opposite. I think it's perfect."

"Me too." I walked into his embrace. "It's like a grown-up night-light. Maybe it will keep the nightmares away."

But I felt too weary to wait until nighttime to find out. I curled up beneath the branches of my own protective tree, images of Jesus' face watching over me as I slept dreamlessly for a couple of hours. My first decently peaceful sleep in three days.

At least I'd gotten one thing right about the cemetery. Trees were a good thing.

And oh, what joy, and what marvelous light
I did behold; yea, my soul was filled with joy
as exceeding as was my pain!
....There could be nothing so exquisite and so bitter
as were my pains. ... On the other hand, there can be
nothing so exquisite and sweet as was my joy.

ALMA 36:20–21

28

LIGHT

A FLORIST DELIVERED three more large bouquets and a couple of potted baskets that afternoon, and when I walked into the living room to read the little cards and find out who they were from, I found Dad and Travis on either end of the black leather couch rearranging furniture to make room for the abundance of floral condolences that continued to arrive.

The incredible array of colors, shapes, and textures had turned my front room into a mini Garden of Eden. But as the hundreds of lily pods were coaxed open by the sunny window, their combined fragrance became hilariously over-intoxicating, and Mom often had to crack open a few windows to keep everyone from feeling faint.

We spent the remaining afternoon hours checking items off the funeral to-do list as quickly as Travis and I had strength and attention for them. I took breaks when needed, and sheltered under my Jesus tree to recoup. But every time I let myself rest, my mind flew back to the cemetery, to the edge of that dreaded pit. I couldn't keep away. And it was driving me mad with despair.

Travis talked me into helping him choose pictures for a memory video he wanted to create for Elora's viewing. We were sitting side by side in the basement in front of the computer screen, laughing and crying over pictures of our girl when the doorbell rang again.

Because Travis and I were in the middle of such a tender project, I waited for someone upstairs to answer the door, but when the bell rang a second time, I walked up the stairs and opened it myself.

Multiple voices cheered, "Surprise!"

I threw the door open wide, ran barefoot down the cement steps, and enfolded three siblings, one sister-in-law, and four nieces and nephews into a giant group hug.

Knowing that all my siblings would arrive sometime that night, Mom had secretly planned a family dinner for me.

Brian's plane had landed safely.

Alicia had braved the Greyhound bus.

And Michael, Deanna, and kids had survived the blizzard.

Their energy was electric, and I cried my first happy tears in days as they came into the house chittering and chatting, piling shoes and coats next to the door and hugging and hugging.

Mom and Dad hurried into the room and joined in. My kids reunited with their cousins and instantly stole them away downstairs to play. The adults congregated in the kitchen, helping take food from the fridge and setting out paper plates and plastic cutlery.

The jovial chatter was refreshing, and for a moment I let all of my worries blow away, allowing myself to be cradled in the familiarity of my family's love.

Halfway through dinner, Rachel and Clark arrived from

Idaho. They called "Hello!" as they came through the door, and we all jumped up from our seats as they appeared in the kitchen.

After hugs all around, Rachel took my arm and led me back into the front room. "I have something for you."

From behind her pile of luggage, she lifted a package wrapped in brown paper and handed it to me. I slipped off the gold ribbon and tore open the wrapping to reveal a beautifully framed print of Jesus holding a child, a little girl with familiar shoulder-length auburn hair and big blue eyes.

I breathed in sharply and looked into my sister's eyes with a question she'd anticipated.

"Clark saw it in the store, and I couldn't believe it when he showed it to me. It's like the artist used Elora as a model. We had to buy it for you."

It was her. My Elora. In heaven, in the arms of the Savior. As if an angel with a camera had spotted a candid moment between Elora and Christ, snapped a picture, and sent me a heavenly postcard.

I kissed Rachel's cheek and held her in a long embrace, then took the picture to my room, closed the door, and sat in my rocker, where I could stare at the framed scene in private. The light of my tree illuminated the joyful little face painted to look so much like my girl.

You little sweetness. Are you happy there?

There. In heaven. That's where she existed now. Yes, her body was still here, on earth. But her spirit, her personality—those were safe in heaven. I stared at the picture while my mind re-evaluated the terror of burying Elora. I stood again at the edge of that pit, but now I could finally hear the answer to the question I'd asked God at the cemetery.

Did we choose the right spot? Will this eventually be a place where my family will feel peace?

Staring at the happy painted scene, I was reassured that when her body was lowered into the ground, Elora would not feel the darkness, or the cold, because she was safe and warm and wrapped in Jesus' arms.

And at that moment, so was I.

His love filled me, shining from every painting of His face on my tree and the new painting in my hands, softening the fear encased around my heart until it melted like candle wax and dripped away.

I displayed the picture on my nightstand beside Elora's yellow seersucker pajamas, and finally, as I rejoined the party, I left the cemetery behind.

29

GIFTED

ONCE DINNER was cleaned up, the family moved to the living room. I sat on the floor, my back against the couch, shoulder to shoulder with my sisters. Mom snuggled up against Dad while he softly played the guitar. Brian kept the conversation flowing light and easy while Clark bounced Noah in his lap. Michael kicked my foot and when I looked at him, he and Deanna just smiled. No one expected anything from me, or asked what they could do. They sat with me and bathed me in love. And I sponged up every second.

While Travis was in the basement checking on the children, there was a knock at the door. Thinking it was the last of my siblings, Lance, arriving from the airport, I leaped across the pile of politely removed shoes and threw open the door.

But it wasn't Lance. I had never seen the woman who stood on the porch, but from her right hand hung a child-sized hanger draped with the most beautiful white satin size 3T dress with simple pearl trim.

"Marianne?"

She smiled shyly. "Krista?"

"Yes! Please, please come in!"

Marianne stepped into the room, and the whole family greeted her. The story of her personal loss and determination to pay forward a kindness had touched them all deeply.

Marianne blushed under the sudden and surely unexpected attention. Focusing back on me, she held up the dress and asked, "What do you think?"

I touched the satiny fabric and the sweet little pearls that circled the neckline, examined the perfectly puffed sleeves and the evenly spaced pleats around the empire waist. I couldn't have found a more perfect dress for Elora if I'd visited dozens of shops.

"It's exquisite."

Marianne blushed more deeply.

I passed the dress to my mom and sisters, who were eager to have a closer look.

Marianne handed me a plastic grocery sack. "There was a little fabric and trim left over. Just in case you need it for anything."

I hugged her. "I know you understand when I say 'thank you' isn't enough. But thank you. I honestly didn't know how I was going to do this part."

"Yes. I *do* know." We smiled at each other. A knowing look formed by common scars. And then the attention was too much for her, and with one last hug, Marianne left.

I retrieved the dress and held it up, stress deflating from my chest like an untied balloon. It was here, in my hands, real and beautiful.

But its beauty was also laced with sadness. This dress would never spin or flounce or flow in the wind as little girls' dresses should. And again, I wished this white dress had been made for any other occasion.

At least she'll look like an angel.

Mom picked up her notebook from the coffee table and flipped to the page of things we needed to buy for the funeral. "We have the dress, slip, tights, and shoes. Now there's only one problem left to solve."

I nodded. "The hat."

I wanted something to cover the scar on Elora's head—a white hat or scarf—but in all our shopping, I hadn't found anything like that. It concerned me that if people saw her stapled scar, it might be shocking, even frightening. And that wasn't the final impression I wanted them to have of my sweet girl. A head covering would allow the focus to remain on her beautiful smile.

Deanna, sitting quietly on the couch beside Michael, suddenly perked up. "What kind of hat?"

I did my best to describe the vision in my mind. "Something to match the style of the dress that covers her head pretty well, but will still show off the hair she has left. I keep thinking about a vintage bouffant hat that poofs out…like a muffin top. Think Little Miss Muffet without the ruffle. Know what I mean?"

"I think so." Deanna stood and took the plastic bag out of my hands, examining the fabric remnants. "With a solid hatband around her forehead?"

"Yeah. Something like that," I said.

"I bet we could make one." Deanna held up the scraps. "There's probably enough fabric left over."

"Really?"

"At least we could try."

"You know when you say *we,* you're really talking about *you,* right?" I nudged her playfully.

Her confidence faltered for a second while she considered the weight of the task. But in a flash, it was back. "I'll drive over to Peggy's, and between the two of us, I'm sure we can figure it out." Our aunt, a talented quilter, would have all the equipment Deanna needed.

An image of Elora's scar flashed in my mind, raw and painful. The hat was vital.

"Honestly, Deanna, I think I've run out of other options. If you can figure this out, it will be a huge blessing."

Mike and Deanna left for Peggy's house at the same time Travis and I left for an appointment with Kiddie Kandids Photography Studio. I'd called that morning and asked if we could buy the copyright to my favorite picture of Elora to use for her obituary and funeral program. We'd arranged to pick up the signed copyright waiver and a digital copy of the photo that evening after the store closed.

Travis and I arrived at the local mall as most of the stores were lowering their metal security gates. Kiddie Kandids had theirs half lowered, signaling they were closed, but still waiting for us. We ducked under the gate, and a young woman with shoulder-length brunette hair greeted us. "Are you the Isaacsons?"

"Yes," I answered.

She clapped her hands together. "Wait here!" Then she hurried down the studio hallway through a door in the back wall.

Confused by the woman's excitement, Travis and I took a seat at the counter on round bubblegum-pink vinyl stools. A few moments later, the young brunette exited the back room, accompanied by two more women. They walked briskly toward us, beaming, each with a load in her arms.

What in the world? We'd come for a signed copyright waiver and a CD with a single picture. *What are they holding?*

They lined up behind the counter, and the older of the three, the manager, said, "When we heard about the loss of your daughter and started looking up her pictures, we couldn't let you leave here with just one. My employees and I have been working all day on a special project. Several of the girls even stayed and worked after their shifts so we could give you this gift."

The women laid their items on the counter. Travis and I stood to get a better look.

First, the manager laid out an 11x13 print of my favorite picture of Elora—the one I'd called to request—finished with a lovely brushstroke varnish, framed in cherry wood.

Second, the quiet blonde employee presented a stack of labeled CDs, a collection of every picture Kiddie Kandids had ever taken of Elora. Five different photo shoots—newborn, baby blessing, 1st birthday, 2nd birthday, and…an impromptu photo session I'd completely forgotten about.

Three months earlier, I'd brought Elora with me to the studio for Noah's newborn photoshoot. We'd been the first ones in the store that day, and a manager had asked to borrow Elora to train a new employee to work with toddlers. I'd grimaced at Elora's crazy bangs and grubby T-shirt, but shrugged my shoulders and said, "Why not?"

I had no idea those would be the last professional photos ever taken of Elora. I hadn't even looked at them that day. But the final gift, laid out by the brunette employee, finally gave me that chance.

On the counter lay five long rectangular-framed custom

collages of Elora's photo shoots, lovingly designed and decorated. This was the work that had taken these ladies all day. The work that had kept them overtime. The reason they didn't want us to arrive until after closing.

Speechless and crying, I examined each frame, each picture, watching Elora grow up before my eyes. And when I got to the last frame, I could barely breathe. There she was, almost exactly like she'd looked the last time I saw her awake. Pictures I had dismissed, that I'd never planned to see. And now, those crazy-haired, grubby-T-shirt pictures were the most precious of all.

Elora's Impromtu Photo Shoot — Kiddie Kandids
November 2006

From over my shoulder, Travis's breath stuttered, and I realized he was crying too.

He said, "I didn't come with Krista to any of these photo shoots. I've never seen most of these pictures, only the few Krista bought. I didn't know I'd ever get the chance to see them all. Thank you."

The three women beamed through their tears. The manager said, "There has been an amazing feeling here today while we worked on this project. Your daughter was here with us. She's such a beautiful girl. We all felt that."

These women who had never met Elora had grown to love her. They'd mourned all day for her loss and were filled with the joy of service.

"Thank you," I said, aware for the second time that evening of the gross understatement of those words. But then I had an idea. "Is there anything you would like to know about her?"

The women glanced at one other conspiratorially before the young brunette answered, "We've been wondering all day what happened to her. But we absolutely don't want to pry."

It was exactly what I'd hoped—a way to show my gratitude. "We'd be honored to tell you."

Travis and I sat again as we relayed Elora's story, from the moment of her first seizure until the moment we came home from the hospital without her. The women listened and cried with us. And when we were finished, they loaded our arms with their gifts and hugged us.

Before we left, the manager added a signed copyright release for every one of Elora's photos. As we walked away, I shouted thank-yous until the women were out of earshot, then cried the rest of the way back to the car. I couldn't wait to show everyone at home the photos of Elora and add them to the box of display items for the funeral.

Travis opened the car's back door. "Krista, I'm honestly blown away," he said as he took the frames out of my arms and spread them single-layer over the seat to keep them safe. "I keep thinking we've seen the best of people, but I continue to be surprised. There's so much good in this world."

"*So* much good," I echoed. "It's what's keeping me going."

Travis opened my door, helped me in, then walked around to the driver's seat and started the ignition. "We're pretty close to Peggy's house. Want to give Deanna a call and see how the hat's coming along?"

"Yes, I do," I said.

Deanna answered her phone right away. "We're almost done," she said. "I hope it's what you wanted. Do you want to stop by and make sure?"

"Yeah," I said. Travis was already headed in the right direction. "We'll be there in a few."

Peggy, Deanna, and Michael were outside waiting in the driveway for us. I hugged my aunt and thanked her for letting us send Deanna over.

"Just wait until you see what she's come up with," Peggy said.

Deanna held up a satin muffin-top hat, exactly as I'd imagined. But then she turned it around, and the back was like no hat I'd ever seen. The hatband was left open, the two sides un-joined, and the back of the muffin top sewn into a triangle point.

Deanna explained, "We didn't know how big Elora's head is, so the hat needed to be adjustable. At first, we couldn't figure out a design that would work, and we knew we'd only get one shot because there was so little fabric left over. There was no room for mistakes. But after I prayed, it was like a blueprint appeared in my head and I knew exactly how to do it."

She demonstrated how the hatband sides and the triangle tip could be adjusted to the right size, and the whole thing secured with a safety pin.

"Deanna, this is brilliant," I said. A pattern sent to her from heaven and executed flawlessly. Stepping closer to the driveway's exterior lighting, I turned the hat over and over, amazed by the clever design. "It's exactly right."

I hugged Deanna, and she exhaled in relief.

I tucked the white satin hat into a plastic bag for safe transportation home, my final worry about the funeral alleviated. Elora's scar would be safely concealed.

Peggy waved from the driveway until we turned the corner out of her neighborhood, Mike and Deanna following closely behind us.

As we drove, I thought of all the people who had used their unique gifts and talents to bless our family. It had been a day full of blessings, but the day wasn't over, and when we arrived home, the evening still had one final gift to deliver.

My brother Lance had finally arrived, and when I walked in the door, my extended family joined in a complete family hug. I bowed my head and closed my eyes, thanking heaven that they had all arrived safely. I held the hug tight for as long as they let me. And even after everyone let go, I knew in my heart that they were all still there, holding on.

For I will fulfil my promises
which I have made unto the children of men . . .

2 NEPHI 10:17

30

READY OR NOT

THAT NIGHT, I held Elora in my dreams.

She sucked her two middle fingers, cradled in my arms while I rocked for hours, nuzzling her downy cheek. She kept trying to leave, but I begged her over and over to stay for a few more minutes.

Then a light shone in my face, sunshine through my bedroom window, and as sleep faded, the dream did too. I cried with my eyes closed, begging God to let me recapture the vision and feeling of holding my little girl, but it evaporated like morning mist in the sun.

She was gone.

I sat up, wrapped my empty arms around myself, and rocked my aching heart side to side.

Mom knocked on the door to see if I was awake, and when I called for her to come in, she sat on the bed, brushing hair from my forehead and a few lingering tears from my cheeks.

"You ready?" she asked.

Today I would get to see Elora, but not like in my dream. She was waiting on me, but not for kisses and snuggles. Today,

Elora needed me to dress her for the last time.

"No," I answered, "I'm not ready. But she needs her mama whether I'm ready or not." And Mom and I sat together and cried.

A generous friend had paid for the gift of a house cleaning service that was scheduled for nine a.m., so Mom helped me gather all of Elora's special white clothes and the supplies I wanted, then we left Travis and Dad in charge of a kids' outing and everyone left just as the cleaners arrived.

Travis's mom, Kathy, and stepmom, Lula, were waiting in the lobby of the Warenski Funeral Home when Mom and I walked in. I had invited all three of Elora's grandmothers to help me pamper her for the last time.

Mr. Warenski had a room prepared for us with Elora already waiting inside. She lay serenely elevated on the same wheeled bed, covered in the same warm blanket. Mom and I let Kathy and Lula approach her, grief washing over them as they greeted her for the first time since her passing.

Mom helped me unpack Elora's clothes and accessories, the hair tools and nail polish. And when Kathy and Lula were ready, I went to Elora's side.

"Hi, baby girl. Mama's here." A warmth spread from my heart, tingling over my skin, and I smiled. Of course Elora wouldn't miss out on this special girl-time. She'd come to make sure her final makeover was perfect.

We started with Elora's tights and ballet slippers. Those were easy enough to get on. But it took all four of us working in tandem to put on her slip and dress. When I finally zipped up the back of the beautiful dress made by Marianne, everyone smiled because it fit Elora perfectly.

Next, Mom helped me roll ringlets into Elora's hair with a curling iron while Kathy and Lula used cotton pads and nail polish remover to take off the chipped peachy polish I'd applied to her nails a couple of weeks ago. But remembering that Shaustia had the same polish on her nails and how proud she was of that connection, I asked the grandmas to leave a few peachy flecks on Elora's left pinkie to show Shaustia at the viewing. Once the rest of Elora's nails were clean and filed, I painted them with a simple coat of clear gloss.

As we worked, Elora's happy spirit filled the room, turning our labor sweet. We chatted and laughed and shared memories of Elora. I knew she was listening and laughing right along with us.

I released the last ringlet from the curling iron and ran my fingers through her hair, knowing it would be my last chance. "I'm so glad the doctor didn't shave it all," I said.

"And it's on the right side, too," Lula said. "When she's in the casket, this is the side that everyone will view her from, so they'll all be able to see her curls."

It was a small happiness to hold on to, but it was enough.

I fluffed and hair-sprayed the ringlets, and when I was finished, Mom picked up Deanna's Little Miss Muffet hat. Careful not to muss her curls, I lifted Elora's head while Mom placed, adjusted, and pinned the hat.

I draped Elora's hair over her right shoulder, pleased with the effect. No one would ever suspect that beneath the little satin muffin top hid an awful, stapled scar. They would only see Elora's smile, just like I'd hoped.

And then, there were only the final touches left.

I fastened a small pearl bracelet around Elora's right wrist, a final gift from me.

And very last, I pinned the white ribbon corsage from her baby blessing to the right side of her hatband.

I stood back to survey our work.

"Perfect," I declared, and my heart disintegrated knowing I had completed my final act of motherly care for Elora's physical body.

I patted her folded hands. "Happy?" I asked her. "I hope so. Because you look like an angel."

I tried not to cry as Mom drove us home, but the tears leaked out anyway.

The cleaners were driving away as we pulled up to the house. I was sorry I'd missed thanking them in person, but settled for a grateful wave, happy they noticed and waved back.

I walked into the house through the garage door, straight into a lemony-fresh kitchen. The whole room sparkled—floors, countertops, table, stove, blinds. The cleaners had touched every inch. In my grieving state, it would have taken me days to accomplish what they had in a few hours.

I hung my purse on its hook and wandered into the living room, greeted by fresh vacuum lines on the carpet and orange oil polish on the banister. The blinds were raised, bathing the wall-to-wall flower arrangements in streak-free midday sunshine that had coaxed dozens more of the sleeping lilies open. I plopped down on the couch, weary, broken-hearted, but thankful for a miraculously clean home. A layer of cobwebs dusted from my soul.

Travis, Dad, and the kids returned home a short time later, and I gathered my children up, smothering them with kisses before they could escape to play. Shaustia asked me to read her a book, and while we enjoyed a few delicious "Red Fish, Green

Fish" moments together, I held her hand, rubbing chippy remnants of peach nail polish with my thumb.

After lunch, Travis, my parents, and I went to the church to set up the funeral display items so everything would be ready for the morning.

Quite a few cars were parked in the church's parking lot, and I hoped there wasn't an activity going on that would delay our set-up plans. But when we walked into the building, I discovered that dozens of neighbors had gathered to prepare the building for Elora's funeral—wiping the glass doors, vacuuming, cleaning the bathrooms and kitchen, polishing pews, washing chalkboards, dusting baseboards, no surface left untouched.

As I walked past them, I thanked them with all the sincerity I could squeeze into words. They didn't halt their work or say much in return, but simply smiled at me with love.

Travis and Dad set up a television in the hallway outside the room where the public viewing would take place so those in line could watch Elora's memory video. Mom and I decorated several display tables with pictures, toys, and trinkets, anything that told a piece of Elora's short but beautiful life story. The funeral director would help us with finishing touches in the morning. But for now, I was pleased and relieved.

Everything was prepared for Elora's funeral.

The family viewing would begin in a couple of hours, and ready or not, the only thing left to do was figure out how to say goodbye.

For thou art my lamp, O Lord:
and the Lord will lighten my darkness.

2 SAMUEL 22:29

31

BRIDGES

Elora was already in Mr. Warenski's viewing room when we arrived for the family viewing. The comfortable room was decorated with crystal chandeliers, breezy curtains, and plush floral carpet. Small groupings of hard-backed chairs had been strategically arranged, and peaceful instrumental music played in the background.

While my parents and siblings unloaded floral arrangements from their cars and helped Mr. Warenski set up stands around the casket for their display, Travis and I escorted our children to see their sister.

Elora's white casket lay in front of a lace-framed picture window with a breathtaking view of pink mountains reflecting the setting sun. Her head rested on a satin pillow that perfectly matched her dress and hat, her auburn curls cascading over her shoulder.

Travis hadn't yet seen Elora dressed in her burial clothes." Wow, she's beautiful. She just looks...asleep."

Caleb, Shaustia, and Walker (on tiptoe) peered over the edge of the child-sized casket.

"Isn't she an angel?" I asked them.

Mr. Warenski had placed a single pink Peruvian lily in Elora's folded hands and applied a delicate layer of makeup to her face—rosy blush, frosty pearl eyeshadow, and light pink gloss on her gently smiling lips.

"Can we touch her?" Shaustia asked.

"Of course," I said.

Travis lifted Walker so he could reach, and they all took turns patting Elora's arms and hands. I showed Shaustia the tiny bit of peachy polish left on Elora's pinkie finger, and she smiled.

With his hand still on his sister's, Caleb asked, "Mom? Can Elora hear us?"

"*I* think she can, but what do *you* think?"

"Yes," he said as he leaned his chin on the edge of the casket close to Elora's face and stroked her arm. "Elora, Budders is here."

Budders. Elora's nickname for Caleb, her pronunciation of the word "brother."

Shaustia and Walker followed Caleb's lead, telling Elora how much they missed her and loved her. Even in death, Elora was still just their sister, and they were not afraid.

Baby Noah squirmed in my arms.

Unlike his siblings, he would have no memory of this moment. No memory of Elora at all. He wouldn't remember how often she'd poked him awake because she wasn't allowed to hold him if he was sleeping. Wouldn't recall the time he'd wailed after she picked him up off the couch, dropped him, and then tattled on herself. "Him heavy!" He wouldn't remember the sound of Elora's voice, or the way her cheek dimpled when she smiled.

Noah would need a bridge. A pathway of stories and pictures

and memories guiding him to a relationship with a sister who had loved him and always would. And who else would be a faithful steward of that bridge if not me? As Noah grew, it would be my responsibility to share every piece of Elora that lived in my head and heart with him.

A knot formed in my throat.

Every piece of Elora.

I looked into her motionless face, her unopened eyes, her silent lips, and wept for all the undiscovered pieces of my little girl. All of the things she hadn't grown old enough to tell me and show me, all of the things she hadn't learned to do, and be, and love. The numberless seeds of her developing personality that would never have the chance to blossom.

As her mother, I knew her better than anyone in the world, and yet...

How well can you know a two-year-old?

What did she dream about?

Did she have a favorite color?

A favorite kind of music?

Was she born with an inclination toward art? Or dance? Or writing?

Noah would have so many questions about her. So did I. Questions that would remain answerless until a day distant in the future when I would again hold her in my arms and finally know Elora the way I longed to.

"Grandma and Grandpa are here," Shaustia said.

Travis's parents had arrived. Travis and the kids went to the foyer to greet them. I lingered another minute at Elora's side, knowing I might not get another chance that evening. As more guests began to arrive, I placed a kiss on my thumb, pressed it to

Elora's chin, and took my designated place beside Travis at the foot of Elora's casket.

It was time for goodbye to begin.

Travis held my hand, and together we breathed in deeply and slowly exhaled. I'd never been the person standing beside a casket greeting guests. The role was a mystery—how to act, what to say. I was concerned about the stamina of my still-recovering body and the frailty of my heart. But mostly, I worried that our guests would look into my eyes and see only exhaustion and sorrow when my heart longed to show my courage and faith.

Heavenly Father, please stand with me, and with my Travis. Teach us what to do.

For the next three hours, God answered my prayer as Travis and I received the strength and courage to greet hundreds of family members who had come to pay their respects to our little girl.

They came in droves, filling the room with conversation, laughter, and hugs. All of our grandparents, parents, siblings, nieces, and nephews were there. Most of our aunts and uncles, dozens of cousins, and many, many more extended family members came from around the country, just as my mother had said they would.

Over and over again, I was moved to tears as beloved, unexpected faces came through the line. The spirit of togetherness, of shared grief, unfailing support, and unconditional love burned so brightly that the air practically glowed.

And I knew the room was even more full with loved ones we could not see—Elora bridging the space between the reunion taking place in that room and the one she was having in heaven.

I gazed around the room, at the smiles wet with tears, the broken hearts filled with faith, and realized that my worries had been unfounded. My heart was allowed to hold both ache and hope simultaneously, and allowing others to witness my sorrow would never negate my faith.

The relatives were slow to leave, drawing out every treasured minute of togetherness. But tonight was not the end. There was still one more day. One final day.

Who shall separate us from the love of Christ?
shall tribulation, or distress, or persecution,
or famine, or nakedness, or peril, or sword?
... Nay, in all these things we are more than conquerors
through him that loved us.

ROMANS 8:35, 37

32

GOODBYE

I STOOD IN MY CLOSET in my pajamas, staring at the row of dresses and skirts. I understood why people traditionally wore black to funerals, but I couldn't bear it if today's sole focus was on grief. Without hope, I would not survive the day.

I removed a black ankle-length skirt from its hanger. Then its matching top—black as well—except the dark background of the shirt was overlaid with red roses. I slipped on the outfit and examined myself in the mirror.

Black for sorrow. Flowers for hope.

It would do.

Mom had already started dressing the children in their Sunday best. Once everyone was pronounced acceptable, she and I opened her notebook list of to-do's. Each item had been checked and double-checked, but I wanted to check one last time.

Every task was complete. There was nothing left to hide behind or distract from the inevitable.

It was time to go.

Our family knelt together in the family room while Travis offered a prayer. "Please bless us all with comfort today, and let

241

us feel Elora around us. Help her to know with certainty how much we love her."

The drive to the church was scarcely five minutes. A charcoal-gray hearse was parked outside the church's east doors. Travis parked the van a few stalls away, and we all soberly walked past it into the church.

Members of the women's Relief Society organization scurried in and out of the gym and kitchen, setting up tables and preparing mountains of food for the family luncheon after the service. Wafts of cheesy funeral potatoes drifted through the hallways, and though they were my favorite, my stomach wasn't the least tempted.

In the foyer outside the chapel, my Aunt Peggy and her daughters had set up a table with pink cardstock and black ink pens for guests to record memories of Elora or write a message to the family.

Mr. Warenski had placed funeral programs and guest sign-in books on tables by both sets of chapel doors and roped off a section of the pews for the family. He'd transported all of the flower arrangements we'd left at the funeral home and decorated the building with them.

I walked down the hallway flanked by my family, past the display tables to the classroom set aside for Elora's second viewing. Once again, Elora was already waiting inside. But today, the lower half of her casket was closed, adorned by a lovely bouquet of white lilies and pink and white roses—the flowers Travis and I had ordered for our girl.

My friend Shannon, one of the women helping prepare the food, noticed we had arrived and brought her camera into the room.

"Hey, you guys," she said as she hugged me and Travis. I introduced her to my parents, who straightway took the kids to find the nursery room and play with the toys.

"Shan, thanks for doing this." Shannon was a fantastic photographer and I'd asked if she would be willing to take some pictures of Elora.

"You bet. I haven't seen Elora yet. Is it okay if I go say hello?"

"Of course," I said.

Shannon began to cry before she'd fully crossed the room to the casket. She stood in silence for a few minutes, looking at Elora's sweet face, struggling to maintain her composure. Then she turned to us and asked, "Is it all right if I start?"

We nodded.

Shannon spent a tearful half hour taking pictures of Elora. Close-ups of her hands and face, full-length pictures of her casket and flowers. Pictures I wasn't sure I'd ever want to look at but had decided that in the long run, I'd rather *have* the pictures and never look at them than *wish* someday for pictures that didn't exist. Shannon had promised to deliver them in a lidded photo-safe box so I could tuck them away and only look if I wanted to.

As Shannon was finishing, a neighbor of ours came to play hymns on the piano, and soon after, the guests began to arrive. Dad started Elora's memory video out in the hallway, and once again, Travis and I took our places next to Elora.

Friends and family filled the halls, many hundreds of people from every place and time period of our lives—childhood friends, college roommates, mission companions, neighbors new and old, our family pediatrician, staff from Elora's hospital stay, Travis's employers and work family, former church leaders, and so many more.

For three hours we greeted them, overwhelmed by the strength and support they brought with them. For most, it was the first time they'd seen us since Elora died, and I was amazed at how many had been holding back their grief, waiting to shed tears until they were with us face-to-face.

I held a box of Kleenex in my arms as I hugged our guests, the tissues as much for their use as for mine. Twice my mother replaced the box. So many people were willing to mourn with me, to hold me, and stand beside me in my pain. I was overcome by the goodness surrounding me.

The time for the funeral program to begin came and went, and still the halls were lined with visitors waiting to greet us and see Elora. Mom knew I wouldn't be satisfied until I'd seen them all, but we couldn't delay the funeral any longer. She suggested that Travis and I go to them.

Mom walked the line ahead of us, explaining and apologizing on our behalf. Travis and I walked behind her, hugging and quickly greeting each person. Once we'd reached the end of the line, we asked our guests to find seats in the chapel. Then Travis and I followed Mom back into the viewing room, where we invited our relatives to stay for the family prayer.

My dad closed the door. Even with most people standing, the room was packed. Everyone who had attended the family viewing the night before was there, plus a few more. Dad stood beside Elora's casket and bowed his head. Everyone followed suit. Dad thanked Heavenly Father for the gift of being Elora's family, for her life, and for the lessons we were all learning from her loss. He asked for God to pour out peace upon us. And he asked that we would always remember to cherish our loved ones.

After the prayer, Travis invited anyone who wanted a last

moment with Elora to approach the casket. Our parents all took turns, tearfully whispering their final words of love.

Then Travis and I gathered our children one last time at Elora's side. Walker, who had yet to cry over his sister, began to sob as his little five-year-old soul finally felt the first stings of death.

We formed a family circle, arms around each other, Travis and I with our hands on Elora's, then we all squeezed each other tight and in our best two-year-old voices mimicked Elora, calling out in unison, "Luz you!" And suddenly I could feel her there. Bright and happy. Elora's sweet spirit had come to join in that final earthly hug. Muffled sobs around the room told me that other people could feel her too.

Granny stood and unfolded a pink crocheted blanket. She'd asked permission to make a blanket for Elora because she couldn't bear the thought of her being cold.

Gramps helped Granny spread the blanket over Elora's legs and arms, and then, though he tried not to be seen, I noticed him slip a sealed envelope into the corner of the casket beside Elora's feet. My stoic, military-vet grandfather, who had suffered the loss of two of his own daughters, had written a letter no one but Elora would ever read.

I passed Noah to my parents, then Travis grasped my hand and together we stood for one last look at our precious one, both trying with all our might to strengthen each other as our hearts simultaneously tore open. Standing surrounded by those who loved us most, Travis and I wept over our daughter. We held her hands and kissed her cheeks, and left tear drops on her skin. We whispered our promise that one day we would be with her again. I unpinned the white ribbon corsage from her hatband and held it over my heart. Then, with a nod from me, Travis reached up to close the lid of the casket.

But he didn't.

He couldn't.

Travis lurched forward, pressed his forehead to Elora's, and sobbed. I rested my hand on his trembling shoulder and let him cry. Those in the room bowed their heads in reverence and respect for a father's grief, most weeping with him.

With a final kiss on Elora's cheek, the last she would receive in this lifetime, Travis stood and slowly lowered the casket lid over our baby's body.

I watched the crack grow smaller until her face disappeared, and then, as the lid fell fully closed with a soft thud, I pressed my tear-filled eyes shut and let that last glimpse of Elora's face burn into my memory.

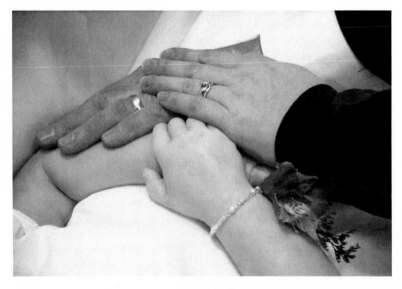

A Last Goodbye
January 24, 2007

Mr. Warenski and an assistant wheeled Elora's casket down the church's hallway through the doors to the chapel. Travis, our kids, and I walked closely behind, followed by the rest of the family. The guests in the chapel stood out of respect while our friend Cheryl played reverent hymns on the organ. The family filed into the reserved pews at the front of the chapel. Once everyone had a place, Bishop Gast asked the congregation to sit, and the funeral began.

I sat on the pew directly in front of Elora's casket, staring at the white lilies and pink roses covering the lid.

How did I get here? How can it be my Elora in that box?

My mind slowed, strength seeping from my arms and hands as shock snaked its way through my body.

Cheryl played the opening notes of "I Am a Child of God." I sang along, missing notes and words as I struggled to keep enough air in my lungs.

Travis's stepdad, Dee, offered the opening prayer, and then Travis's stepmom, Lula, and mom, Kathy, shared memories of Elora. I listened, but found my mind prone to wander.

I will never see her face again. Never touch her again.

My hands trembled, face tingled, impossible heaviness settling into my limbs.

What was I thinking, adding myself to the program? How did I think I would be in any condition to stand and speak?

Something dark and oppressive pressed against my chest.

I sank deeper into my seat as I struggled to breathe.

Panic gripped my throat, heavy and tight. I was trapped. Held captive by darkness.

I nearly reached out my hand to Travis for help.

But at that moment, my mother stood. It was her turn to

speak. She started by sharing her experience of losing two of her own sisters, and then, she began to speak of Christ. A powerful witness and testimony that pierced the darkness like a sword, forcing it from the room. Breath filled my lungs, and the heaviness retreated. And by the time she ended her remarks, my limbs had regained their strength.

I stood.

Armed with a slip of paper with a single scripture and a couple of hastily jotted bullet-point ideas, I approached the pulpit. The crowd filled the chapel and the overflow behind, back so far that I could not see the faces on the last rows.

Two potted lilies had been placed on the corners of the pulpit, hedging me in safely on both sides with their promise of peace.

"You probably think I'm crazy for wanting to speak today," I said to the crowd, "but how could I miss coming up here and seeing this sight? Seeing your faces? You are the reason I am standing."

I shared an experience from my childhood, an elementary school science experiment. My teacher had passed two containers around the room, a large bleach bottle and a small baking soda can. He explained that they both held a measure of sand. Our job was to hold the containers, one in each hand, and determine which was heavier.

The class weighed and discussed and unanimously voted that the little can was heavier than the large bottle.

Our teacher then put the containers on a scale and we discovered with our own eyes that our guess was wrong. The bleach bottle was several ounces heavier than the baking soda can.

"But how?" we asked. The large bottle had felt so much lighter than the can.

"Science," our teacher answered, and then explained that the weight of the small can had been compacted into a small space that fit in the palms of our hands. But the weight of the bleach bottle was dispersed over the entire surface of our hands and beyond. The more surface area to help carry the weight, the lighter the burden.

"And that is what all of you are doing for me," I said. "Each one of you has lightened my burden. You each carry a piece of the weight of losing Elora, and Christ is helping me carry the rest. He said, 'for all flesh is in mine hands; be still and know that I am God' (Doctrine & Covenants 101:16). And that is what I will try to do. Let Elora rest in His hands and be patient, knowing she is cared for, until I can see her again."

When I had finished speaking, I motioned my children forward, then Caleb, Shaustia, and Walker sang two of Elora's favorite Primary songs, "Jesus Wants Me for a Sunbeam" and "I'm Trying to Be Like Jesus."

Travis spoke next, bearing a powerful testimony of Christ's strength and love. Then Bishop Gast spoke of our shared belief that family relationships are perpetuated beyond the grave. And finally, our dear friend and the stake president over our local group of ward congregations, Chris Yadon, gave the closing remarks.

Chris and his wife, Christy, had been part of a babysitting group we'd formed when we'd moved into the area. The Yadons, Allens, Walkers, and Isaacsons had taken turns watching each other's children every Friday for years. Not only had we saved ourselves hundreds of dollars in babysitting fees, but we'd formed deep friendships that more closely resembled family.

Chris spoke about the last time Elora had been in their home, and how he knew that she was a precious daughter of God. I was thankful to be reminded that my Heavenly Father loved Elora even more than I did, and that as much as I was missing her, He was glad to have her home. I thought about that joyful heavenly hug between father and child, and smiled knowing one day I'd get one too.

I leaned over to Travis and whispered in his ear, "I'd better outlive you because if I get to heaven first, I'll get Elora's first hug, and you need to know that once I get ahold of her, I'm never letting go."

Travis chuckled.

We sang the closing hymn, "Families Can Be Together Forever," then Travis's dad, Jeff, closed the meeting with prayer.

The congregation stood as Elora's casket was wheeled down the aisle, our family following closely behind. Over the sound of tears, Cheryl, at the organ, played a hymn. Perhaps no one else in the room noticed that Cheryl had turned the organ pipes to the sound of Christmas bells, but Travis and I did. The bells were Travis's favorite. He told Cheryl after every Christmas Sunday service and she had remembered, blessing our painful recessional with an audible gift of love only he and I would recognize.

He smiled at me, tears puddled under his eyes, and we both glanced back over our shoulders at Cheryl. Her eyes were focused on the music, but the tears fogging her glasses and dripping from her chin said it all.

Outside the church's east doors, the family gathered in the chilly winter sunlight while Elora's casket was lifted into the hearse by the pallbearers—her three grandfathers and two big brothers, Caleb and Walker.

A generous neighbor, the owner of a limousine company, surprised our family with a beautiful ride to the cemetery. It was large enough to accommodate Travis, me, the kids, and all of our parents and grandparents. Caleb, Shaustia, and Walker were overjoyed climbing into the spacious vehicle and instantly started pushing buttons and opening cabinets. Travis handed me a water bottle from the mini fridge and I drank gratefully, watching out the tinted window as dozens of cars, each flashing hazard lights, joined the caravan to the American Fork Cemetery.

The piece of ground we'd purchased beneath the ancient sycamores was covered in green turf fabric with a metal casket-lowering device installed over the previously dug grave. With so many loved ones gathered on the spot, it regained some of the beauty I'd seen there before. I recalled the picture gifted by my sister Rachel, the scene of the little girl sitting with Jesus, smiling, and felt a measure of courage injected into my soul.

Shaustia and I took seats at the graveside with the other women while the pallbearers carried Elora's casket from the hearse and rested it atop the straps over her grave. Mr. Warenski carried the bouquet of lilies and roses and placed it on the casket.

I held my children in my arms while our family and friends gathered tightly around us. Travis stood and offered one final prayer, dedicating Elora's burial place as sacred ground to be protected and blessed with a spirit of peace for all who would visit her there.

We took a few family pictures, and stayed to thank all those not attending the family luncheon. But as the crowd waned and family members made their way back to their cars, I stood for the last time beside Elora's angel-white casket. I plucked a white lily from her bouquet, and then, much like in the hospital, I gave my girl a final kiss—pressed to the lid of her casket—left behind a piece of my heart, turned, and walked away.

It was finished.

The limousine ride back to the church was quiet. I could feel myself riding the final waves of adrenaline and added strength from God, my energy receding like the tide.

Elora's Spot
American Fork Utah Cemetery
January 24, 2007

By the time we arrived back at the church, my body and mind felt numb, distant, slow. Travis held Noah and shepherded the other kids from the limo back into the church. Mom and Dad each took one of my arms and walked me to a table in the gym.

After a blessing on the food, someone loaded up a plate of amazing food and placed it in front of me. I'd barely eaten all day, and the food finally smelled appetizing. I ate a large helping of funeral potatoes, a warm homemade dinner roll dripping with melted butter, and most of my raspberry Jell-O salad, but with my stomach full and my heart empty, I was out of balance, every molecule of my being drenched in weariness.

The room was full of so many people I wanted to visit with, cousins I didn't know if I'd see again for years, but I didn't have the energy to stand and go to them. Thankfully, most of them came to me. I stayed as long as possible, hugging and chatting and thanking, gifting flower arrangements to family members who lived close by. But eventually the effort drained me of my last dregs of strength, and Mom declared it was time to go home.

My siblings retrieved the remaining flower arrangements from around the building while my aunts helped Mom gather items from the display tables and memory book table.

I insisted that Travis steer me past the kitchen so I could thank my friends for the wonderful luncheon. My heart longed to hug each one and thank them personally, but instead I stood in the kitchen doorway, smiled, and blew a kiss to the whole group, hoping they would all feel my love.

Finally, we drove home.

Every muscle in my body ached, including my heart, but I had to conclude that Elora's funeral had far exceeded my hopes for a beautiful, faith-filled celebration of her life. I knelt by my bed and thanked my Father in Heaven for holding me and guiding me through the hardest week of my life. Tomorrow I would face the lifelong work of learning to live without Elora, but tonight, I retrieved her stuffed yellow duck from the pile beside my bed and fell deeply to sleep. Today was finished.

Behold, I have refined thee,
but not with silver;
I have chosen thee in the furnace of affliction.

ISAIAH 48:10

33

Unbearable Burden

After the funeral, Mom stayed for a couple more weeks to help out. She kept the house clean, the kids entertained, and all of us fed. And when I needed something to keep my hands busy, she taught me to crochet.

On the day she left, I stood on the front porch watching her taillights disappear, and then I stayed there longer, crying, as I tried to figure out how I would get along without her, how I'd step back into all of the roles she'd been covering for me.

I told Travis I needed to get away.

Away from the constant reminders of Elora's absence.

Away from the dreary, frigid winter weather.

I needed an anonymous place to think, to refresh, to center myself, and to figure out how to go about living again.

And our family needed time together, just us.

A few days later, Travis and I surprised the kids with a spontaneous trip to California. I packed their bags in secret and woke them as if it were time for school. But instead of driving into the school parking lot, we turned onto the freeway and ended up at the airport. It was their first airplane ride, and they were ecstatic. We played on the beach for five days, allowing sand and sunshine and salty wind to scour away some of the hurt.

Caleb, Shaustia, and Walker greeting the ocean
February 2007

When we arrived back home, we knew it was time to start breaking in our new normal. So Travis went back to work, Caleb, Shaustia, and Walker returned to school, and little by little, the heavenly protective bubble and the phone calls, visits, and meals from friends tapered off.

I'd known the day would come—that it *had* to come—when I'd be left on my own to face the full measure of my grief. I couldn't be carried, distracted, and sheltered forever. Like a newborn deer, my untested legs would only grow strong with use. My grief needed to be worked through. But it was hard, and I struggled.

I missed Elora.

Every day I willed myself out of bed, dressed, helped the children get ready for school, kissed Travis goodbye, and worked in small strides around the house—a load of dishes, a stack of laundry, vacuuming a room—until my energy reserves depleted and I collapsed on the couch with the baby.

Outside my living room window, children rode their bikes in circles around the cul-de-sac, and neighbors walked their dogs and unloaded plastic grocery sacks from the backs of their minivans. How had those small day-to-day things ever felt simple? And would they ever again?

I was as unprepared for the long game of carrying Elora's absence day after day as I had been for the sudden shock of her death. And yet, though the weight of missing Elora burdened me terribly, I could not put her down. I thought about her every second I was awake—drifting through memories of her childhood, berating myself for every instance I'd been an imperfect mother, haunted by scenes from the hospital and my inability to protect her.

Days passed.

Why didn't I just stop what I was doing and read her that book she asked for?

Weeks passed.

Why was I so frustrated when she kissed the baby too hard and woke him?

Months passed.

Why didn't I take her to the doctor sooner? She must have been in so much pain. I didn't know. I didn't see. I didn't help her. Oh…I didn't help her.

Every day, my guilt swelled, bigger and more painful until I could no longer see past it. And though I made an effort to take the kids to the park, attend church on Sundays, and do the weekly grocery shopping, there were also days I didn't make it out of my pajamas. Days I slept as much as I was awake.

Slowly, imperceptibly, I began to believe the scornful voice in my head taunting me that a better mother would have caught Elora's tumor sooner and eased her pain. A better mother would have been more attentive, more in tune. A better mother would have saved Elora.

I'd known people who succumbed to dark places. Their personal devastation wreaked havoc upon everything and everyone around them, spreading through all the precious parts of their lives—family, health, faith—until those things too were destroyed.

I could not let that happen. Would not.

And finally, on a particularly frightening day of spiraling into darkness, I was ready to admit I needed help. Immediate help.

In the hospital and during Elora's funeral, God had shown me countless times that He was with me, and that He would answer my prayers for help.

When was the last time I asked Him for it?

I couldn't remember.

Sitting on the couch in my pajamas, I retrieved my neglected scriptures from the nearby coffee table and opened the Bible to the Topical Guide.

Peace.

It was the first topic that came to my mind. The thing I was most desperate to find.

I searched through the verses listed under the heading for peace and read.

"Peace I leave with you, my peace I give unto you: not as the world giveth, give I unto you. Let not your heart be troubled, neither let it be afraid" (John 14:27).

And, "Come unto me, all ye that labour and are heavy laden, and I will give you rest. Take my yoke upon you, and learn of me; for I am meek and lowly in heart; and ye shall find rest unto your souls. For my yoke is easy, and my burden is light" (Matthew 11: 28-30).

And, "Cast thy burden upon the Lord, and he shall sustain thee" (Psalm 55:22).

I had been trying to carry the burden of Elora's death on my own since her funeral, and it wasn't working very well. But reading those Bible verses reminded me that God had never intended me to carry my burdens alone. That's exactly why He sent Christ to the earth—to help.

But it isn't fair!

Elora's death. All of my mortal motherly mistakes. All of the moments of regret and pain. Those things were not Christ's fault. They were mine. And so, they were mine to carry.

Tendrils of doubt slithered around my heart.

How can I ask Jesus to help carry something that isn't His fault?

I looked down at the scriptures in my hands. My whole life, I'd been taught that when Jesus suffered and died, He experienced every hard thing so that He would know how to help every person bear their heavy burdens.

Burdens exactly like mine.

I needed Him. I couldn't do it without His help. But that meant I had to do my part. If Christ could just come and lift the unbearable things from my shoulders, He already would have.

No.

The instructions in the Bible were clear. I had to be the one to give them up. Sacrifice them. Absolve myself. Let go.

I needed to *cast* them.

Jesus was asking me to give the unbearable things to Him, yoke myself to Him. And I was so desperate for relief, I decided to try it right then, right there.

I stood up from the couch and imagined a backpack on my shoulders. I loaded the pack with all of the unbearable things about Elora's death, all of my guilt and regrets. I cried as I examined each memory before letting them drop into the depths of the pack, out of sight. The imaginary straps grew heavy, digging into the flesh of my heart, reopening the poorly healed wounds. And still, I stuffed more into the pack.

When I finally had nothing left to add and the pack truly felt too heavy to bear another moment longer, I did one of the hardest things I've ever done—I gave myself permission to let it all go. I mimed lifting the pack's straps off my shoulders, off my soul, and I threw my hands out in front of me, casting my burdens to the ground.

I sobbed as I spoke aloud. "My brother Jesus? I can't carry this without help. It's too heavy. I need you. Will you please help me?"

Immediately, I felt His answer. He said yes.

My heart sprang loose from the coils of regret and guilt that had bound it so tightly, reminding me of a favorite Book of Mormon scripture. "And oh, what joy, and what marvelous light I did behold; yea, my soul was filled with joy as exceeding as was my pain!" (Alma 36:20)

That day, Jesus and I lifted my pack together, one strap each, and I discovered His promised rest to my soul as we took our first yoked step on the path leading away from despair back into the light.

Jesus has walked beside me every day since. And I'll need Him at my side for the rest of my life because there are things about Elora's death that will always be too heavy for me to bear alone. I know, because on certain occasions I've mistakenly believed that enough time has passed, that I can safely take a peek inside, that I'm finally strong enough to handle the difficult memories stowed inside the pack without Him. But it only takes a second of holding those burdens alone for me to remember why I asked Christ to help me carry them in the first place.

The beautiful thing about Jesus is that He never belittles or mocks me for making that mistake. He waits patiently for me to remember how much I need Him, and no matter how many times I cast my pack to the floor again and ask Him, "Will you please help me carry this?" He says yes. And He always will.

As long as I continue to invite Him, Jesus will walk beside me helping to bear the loads that are too heavy. Teaching me, strengthening me, and guiding me to resources and opportunities for further healing. And I have learned to love Him, to trust Him, and to rely on Him as a constant companion along my path. He truly "has become my salvation" (2 Nephi 22:2).

The road through grief is a lifelong journey. But I now know that with Christ's help, I can "do all things" (Philippians 4:13).

He makes that same promise to every single one of us, no matter the burdens we carry. Jesus Christ is infinitely loving, infinitely powerful, and infinitely willing to carry it all. It's we who must be brave enough to ask for His help, trusting that with Christ at our side, there is no such thing as an unbearable burden.

Behold, God is my salvation;
I will trust, and not be afraid;
for the Lord Jehovah is my strength and my song;
he also has become my salvation.

2 NEPHI 22:2

ALL IS WELL

I slid a slice of pumpkin pie onto my plate and reached for the tub of Cool Whip. Travis scooped up a piece of his favorite chocolate cream pie, then slipped his arm around my waist.

"Aren't they cute?" He pointed with his chin toward the living room, where my entire extended family sat eating Thanksgiving dessert enthralled by the two newest grandbabies rolling around on the floor.

I smiled. "*So*, so cute."

Travis leaned in close and whispered in my ear, "We should have one."

I spun around to face him, nearly knocking the pie off my plate. It had been years since we last talked of having another baby. I rolled my eyes and smirked, "Very funny," then turned toward the living room to join the baby watching.

But Travis reached for my arm and pulled me back. "No, really. We should."

I set my plate on the table and tried to keep my shock in check. "Honey…I…what?"

"I know, I know. It's just…I keep feeling like we're missing someone."

I nodded. "Me too. Every day."

263

But he shook his head. "Not just Elora."

My brain still hadn't moved past pumpkin pie. I opened and closed my mouth—no words. Travis took advantage of my stupor to plow forward.

"I've been watching the babies this week and missing Elora, and it's weird, but I feel like she's trying to tell us that it's not only her I've been missing. It's like she's been shouting to me from heaven that we forgot someone."

I plopped down in a dining room chair, my back to the family. "But babe...Noah's five. He's going to kindergarten next fall. We're done with diapers and sippy cups, and...we sold the crib, the clothes, everything!"

"Shhh!" He smiled as he motioned for me to keep my voice down.

I blushed, hoping no one had heard, and said, "Why are you smiling?"

"Because I think it's a girl. And her name is Hannah. And I think she needs to come."

I stared at him, dumbfounded. But in his eyes was a little excited sparkle that sent a familiar motherly twinge into my heart. I shook my head, defeated by his charm, and smiled back.

"Krista, just think about it." He stood, kissed my forehead, and picked up his pie. "And pray, too."

That night, with Travis already in bed, I knelt on the floor of my mother's blue-and-white guest room ready to tell Heavenly Father all the reasons I couldn't have another baby—I was getting too old, it would be expensive, the kids needed my full attention, I didn't know if I was ready to open my heart like that again, it would feel like trying to replace Elora, and people would think we were irresponsible or insane...

But I didn't get past "Dear Father in Heaven" before a picture appeared in my head of Elora standing with her arm around a little girl, a giant smile on her face. My heart burst wide, flooded with love for a child who had not yet been born, and all my excuses evaporated. I popped up from the floor like a Jack-in-the-Box, grabbed half-asleep Travis by the leg, and squealed, "A baby!"

Travis just smiled that big, goofy, toothy grin of his.

Fifteen months later, Hannah Helen was born. My smallest baby by far, but so much like Elora. The same mop of dark hair, the same red birthmark in the center of her forehead. Travis and I decided that was where her angel sister had kissed her goodbye before sending her down to us. I placed my lips over the mark, kissing both of my daughters simultaneously.

The night we brought Hannah home, the children gathered around to take turns snuggling her. I looked into the faces of all my precious ones, knowing Elora was there too, and recalled the words that Heavenly Father had sent to me in a blessing all those years ago in the hospital. He'd promised "All will be well." And in that happy moment, I knew I'd arrived. I'd traveled a hard road and finally come to a place where my heart was at peace, the horizon soaked in warm sunlight.

God had kept His promise. All was well.

Hannah Helen Isaacson
February 2013

Isaacson Family
Caleb, Noah, Shaustia, Travis, Hannah, Krista, Walker, Angel Elora
September 2016

ACKNOWLEDGMENTS

M Y FIRST AND MOST HEARTFELT GRATITUDE goes to my Heavenly Father. You have taught me through your gentle, infinite love to do hard things. There was not a single writing session that did not begin in prayer, asking you for courage and direction, and you have given it generously.

To my brother Jesus Christ, who continues even now to walk by my side—without your grace, I never would have survived the darkness. My greatest wish in writing this book has been to guide others to your care.

Travis, this is your story as much as it's mine, and I'm forever grateful for the bond that was forged unbreakable between us in the crucible of grief. Thank you for your constancy, support, encouragement, and love. I look forward with hope to that heavenly hug you and I will one day share with our girl. Lucky are we.

Caleb, Shaustia, Walker, Noah, and Hannah, thank you for your patience every time you needed something from me but I didn't hear you talking because I was writing. Being your mother has filled my life with glorious purpose, and I love you forever.

To all of my parents, siblings, grandparents, family members, and dear friends—you are the army of hands that did not let me fall. Each one of you has added something irreplaceable to my life, and I would not be who I am today, nor would this book exist, without your influence.

To the doctors, nurses, and funeral professionals who dedicated so much time and skill to care for Elora—the worst day of my life was just another day at work for you all, and yet you gave our family so much attention and care. I will never understand the personal courage it takes to daily do what you do. You are all angels on earth.

Special thanks to Annette Lyon, my first mentor, for reading the first draft of my first chapter and igniting a spark of confidence in me that I really could write a book. Voila, my friend!

To the members of the Thursday Three—Michelle and Sabrina—and the Reality Writers—Karin, Rena, Abel, Steve, Carmen, Elizabeth, Allison, Becky, Nannette, JoAnna, Mary, and Tom—thank you with all my heart for the years of reading, critiquing, rereading, crying in all the right places, irreplaceable friendship, and cheering me on to the finish line.

To my beta readers—Brenda, Dave, Lance, Alicia, Robin, and Cory, the first people to read the book cover to cover—thank you for the gifts of your time and polishing skills.

To my mentors, Abel Keogh, Jodi Brown, Tamara Andersen, Chris Shoebinger, Wendy Jessen, and Leta Greene, thank you for lending me your ears every time I had a writing, publishing, or marketing question. I promise to pay your kindnesses forward someday.

To my glorious editor, Tristi Pinkston, thank you for making my manuscript shine while staying true to my voice and experience. But mostly, thank you for rescuing me from comma overuse purgatory. Working with you has been a joy.

To my talented daughter, Shaustia Brown, thank you for the

gorgeous logos and other graphic design work that have become the symbols to represent all of the faith, hope, and love poured into this book.

To my incredible interior and cover designer, Francine Platt at Eden Graphics, you have taken an ugly duckling and turned her into a swan. Thank you for giving my book the visual beauty and order it deserves.

To my photographer Belinda Olsen, I love every chance I get to see the world through your eyes. Thank you for understanding the vision in my head and turning it into reality. But most of all, thank you for the confidence you lent me. Your patient friendship always puts me at ease.

And finally, to my dear one, Elora Lyn, how can I ever thank you for all your too-short life has taught me? I cannot calculate the breadth and depth of your influence. I still sometimes find it hard to wait patiently until the day I will see you again, but when I think of your dimpled smile, it gives me courage to try to live each day in a way that will make you proud of me, that will refine me until I am worthy to be where you are. I dream of the day I can hold you and ask all of my questions—I really want to know your favorite color. Until then, know that you live forever in my heart. Luz you ha, ha. –Mom

ABOUT THE AUTHOR

Krista M. Isaacson is an award-winning writer, founder and president of the Reality Writers online guild for nonfiction authors, and inspirational speaker. But most importantly, she is a felicitously married mother of six children—including a daughter who has earned her angel wings—and professional spoiler of her grandchildren.

Originally from the California Bay area, she and her family currently live in the shadow of Utah's beautiful Wasatch Mountains. She is a lover of vintage boutiques, pumpkin spice, holiday picture books, painting fairy-tale murals, and her mountain bike named Breezy. Her dearest hope is that one day you'll find her in London mudlarking for treasure on the foreshore of the Thames.

Connect with Krista online

 KristaMIsaacson.com

 /KristaMIsaacson

 @KristaMIsaacson

Made in United States
North Haven, CT
04 August 2022

22285511R00169